# Early Literacy

Join us on the web at

**www.cengage.com/education**

# Early Literacy

*Phygenia Young and Ann Watts*

Australia • Brazil • Japan • Korea • Mexico • Singapore • Spain • United Kingdom • United States

**WADSWORTH**
CENGAGE Learning™

**Early Literacy**
**Phygenia Young, Ann Watts**

Editor: Christopher Shortt
Development Editor: Tangelique
   Williams
Assistant Editor: Caitlin Cox
Editorial Assistant: Linda Stewart
Media Editor: Ashley Cronin
Marketing Manager: Kara
   Kindstrom
Marketing Assistant: Dimitri
   Hagnere
Marketing Communications
   Manager: Martha Pfeiffer
Project Manager, Editorial
   Production: Christy Krueger
Creative Director: Rob Hugel
Senior Art Director: Maria Epes
Print Buyer: Becky Cross
Production Service: Graphic World
Compositor: Graphic World

For product information and
technology assistance, contact us at **Cengage Learning
Customer & Sales Support, 1-800-354-9706**

For permission to use material from this text or product,
submit all requests online at **cengage.com/permissions**
Further permissions questions can be emailed to
**permissionrequest@cengage.com**

Library of Congress Control Number: 2005054670

ISBN-13: 978-1-4180-0038-7

ISBN-10: 1-4180-0038-8

**Wadsworth**
10 Davis Drive
Belmont, CA 94002-3002
USA

Cengage Learning is a leading provider of customized learning solutions with office locations around the globe, including Singapore, the United Kingdom, Australia, Mexico, Brazil, and Japan. Locate your local office at: **www.cengage.com/international.**

Cengage Learning products are represented in Canada by Nelson Education, Ltd.

For your course and learning solutions, visit **academic.cengage.com.**

Purchase any of our products at your local college store or at our preferred online store **www.ichapters.com.**

**Notice to the Reader**
Publisher does not warrant or guarantee any of the products described herein or perform any independent analysis in connection with any of the product information contained herein. Publisher does not assume, and expressly disclaims, any obligation to obtain and include information other than that provided to it by the manufacturer. The reader is expressly warned to consider and adopt all safety precautions that might be indicated by the activities described herein and to avoid all potential hazards. By following the instructions contained herein, the reader willingly assumes all risks in connection with such instructions. The publisher makes no representations or warranties of any kind, including but not limited to, the warranties of fitness for particular purpose or merchantability, nor are any such representations implied with respect to the material set forth herein, and the publisher takes no responsibility with respect to such material. The publisher shall not be liable for any special, consequential, or exemplary damages resulting, in whole or part, from the readers' use of, or reliance upon, this material.

Printed in Canada
3 4 5 13 12 11 10 09 08

# CONTENTS

| | |
|---|---|
| Introduction | vii |
| Reflections for Growing Teachers | 1 |
| Tips for Success | 6 |
| Getting Started | 9 |
| Developmental Milestones by Age | 12 |
| Developmental Milestones by Skill | 31 |
| Play Materials for Children | 49 |
| Observation and Assessment | 54 |
| Curriculum and Lesson Plans | 65 |
| Making Connections through Webbing | 72 |
| Understanding the Development of Language and Literacy | 75 |
| Books for Children | 82 |
| Developmentally Appropriate Practice | 95 |
| Guidelines for Developmentally Appropriate Practice | 97 |
| Professional Organizations | 100 |
| Resources | 105 |
| Case Studies | 112 |
| Issues and Trends | 122 |

*This tool was developed to help you, the budding teacher and/or child care provider, as you move into your first classroom. The editors at Wadsworth, a part of Cengage Learning, encourage and appreciate your feedback on this or any of our other products.*

# INTRODUCTION

Throughout a college program of preparation to become an early childhood educator, students take many courses and read many textbooks. Their knowledge grows as they accumulate ideas from lectures, reading, experiences, and discussions. When they finish their coursework, graduate, and move into their first teaching positions, students often leave behind some of the books they have used. The hope is, however, that they will take with them the important ideas from their classes and books as they begin their own professional practice.

More experienced colleagues or mentors sometimes support teachers in their first teaching positions, helping them make the transition between being a student in a college classroom and being responsible for a group of young children. Other times, new teachers are left to travel their own paths, relying on their own resources. Whatever your situation, this professional enhancement guide is designed to provide reminders of what you have learned, as well as resources to help you make sense of and apply that knowledge.

Teachers of young children are under great pressure today. Families are looking for support in their difficult tasks of child-rearing in today's fast-paced and changing world. Some families become so overwhelmed with the tasks of parenting that they seem to leave too much responsibility on the shoulders of teachers and caregivers. Administrators and institutions have expectations that sometimes seem overwhelming. Teachers are being held accountable for children's learning in ways unprecedented in even the recent past. Public scrutiny has led to insistence on teaching practices that may seem contrary to the best interests of children or their teachers. New teachers may find themselves caught between the realities of the schools or centers where they find themselves, and their own philosophies and ideals of working with children. When faced with such dilemmas, it is important for these individuals to be able to fall back and reflect on what they know of best practices, renewing their professional determination to make appropriate decisions for children.

These professional enhancement books provide similar tools for that reflection:

- tips for getting off to a great start in your new environment
- information about typical developmental patterns of children from birth through school age
- suggestions for materials that promote development for children from infancy through the primary grades
- tools to assist teachers in observing children and gathering data to help set appropriate goals for individual children
- guides for planning appropriate classroom experiences and sample lesson plans
- tips for introducing children to the joys of literacy
- a summary of the key ideas about Developmentally Appropriate Practice, the process of decision making that allows teachers to provide optimal environments for children from birth through school age
- resources for teachers for professional development
- ideas for where you can access lists of other resources
- case studies of relevant, realistic situations you may face, as well as best practices for successfully navigating them
- insight into issues and trends facing early childhood educators today

Becoming a teacher is a process of continuing to grow, learn, reflect, and discover through experience. Having these resources may help you along your way. Good luck on your journey!

# REFLECTIONS FOR GROWING TEACHERS

Teachers spend most of their time working with young children and their families. During the day, questions and concerns arise and decisions have to be made, meaning teachers must always be reflective about their work. Too often, teachers believe they are too busy to spend time thinking, but experienced professional teachers have learned that reflection sustains their best work. Growing teachers need to regularly take time to consider the questions and concerns that arise from their practice. Some teachers use journals to keep track of the process.

Use these questions to begin your reflection and then add to them with questions from your own experience. Remember, these are not questions to be answered once and forgotten—come back often.

## QUESTIONS FOR REFLECTION

This day would have been better if _____

_____

I think I need to know more about _____

_____

One new thing I think I will try this week is _____

_____

The highlight of this week was _____

_____

The observations this week made me think more about _____

_____

I think my favorite creative activity this year was _____

_____

One area where my teaching is changing is _____

_____

One area where my teaching needs to change is _____

_____

I just do not understand why _____

_____

I loved my job this week when _____

_____

I hated my job this week when _____

_____

One thing I can try to make better next week is _____

_____

The funniest thing I heard a child say this week was _____

_____

The family member I feel most comfortable with is _____

_____

And I think the reason for that is _____

_____

The family member I feel least comfortable with is _____

_____

And I think the reason for that is _____

_____

The biggest gains in learning have been made by _____

_____

And I think that this is because _____

_____

I am working on a bad habit of _____

_____

Has my attitude about teaching changed this year? _____

Why? _____

What have I done lately to spark the children's imagination and creativity? _____

_____

One quote that I like to keep in mind is _____

_____

Dealing with _____ is the most difficult thing I had to face recently

because _____

My teaching style has been most influenced by _____

_____

In thinking more about early literacy in my curriculum, I believe _____

_____

If I were going to advise a new teacher, the most helpful piece of advice would be

_____

I have been trying to facilitate friendships among the children by _____

_____

I really need to start _____

_____

I used to _____ but now I _____

_____

The child who has helped me learn the most is _____. I learned _____

_____

I have grown in my communication by _____

_____

The best thing I have learned by observing is _____

_____

I still do not understand why _____

_____

One mistake I used to make that I do not make any longer is _____

_____

When next year starts, one thing I will do more of is _____

_____

When next year starts, one thing I will not do is _____

_____

One way I can help my children feel more competent is _____

_____

Something I enjoy that I could share with my class is _____

_____

When children have difficulty sharing, I _____

_____

_____

_____

_____

_____

_____

_____

_____

_____

_____

_____

_____

_____

_____

_____

Adapted from Nilsen, B. A. (2004). *Week by week: Documenting the development of young children* (3rd ed.). Clifton Park, NY: Thomson Delmar Learning.

## TIPS FOR SUCCESS

Remember that you are a role model for the children. They are constantly watching how you dress, what you say, and what you do.

### BE A PROFESSIONAL

- Dress conservatively and follow your employer's clothing expectations (which could include wearing closed-toe shoes to be safe and active with children and wearing clean, modest, and comfortable clothing).

- Be prepared and on time.

- Avoid excessive absences.

- Use appropriate language with children and adults.

- Be positive when talking to parents and show that you are forming a positive relationship with their child; "catch children doing something right" and share those accomplishments. Challenges with children can be discussed after you have established trust with the parents.

### BE A TEAM PLAYER

- Rely on team members to help you learn the parameters of your new position.

- Do not be afraid to ask questions or for guidance from teammates.

- Show your support and be responsible.

- Step in to do your share of the work; do not expect others to clean up after you.

- Be of assistance to others whenever possible.

- Respect others' ideas and avoid telling them how to do things.

- Strive to balance your ability to make decisions with following the lead of others.

## LEARN ABOUT CHILDREN

- Be aware of children's development physically, socially, emotionally, and cognitively.

- Assess children's development and plan curriculum that will enhance it.

- Be aware that children will test you! (Children, especially school-age children, will expect that you do not know the rules and may try to convince you to let them do things that were not previously allowed.)

- Never hesitate to double-check something with teammates when in doubt.

- Use positive management techniques with children.

## MANAGEMENT TECHNIQUES FOR GAINING CHILDREN'S COOPERATION

There are myriad techniques that will help children cooperate. Children need respectful reminders of expectations and adult support in performing to those expectations. Be sure that your expectations are age appropriate and individually appropriate. These techniques are more preventive in nature:

- Use positive phrases and state exactly what you expect children to do. "Stand by the door" is more effective that "Don't go outside until everyone is ready."

- Avoid "no" and "don't." Be clear about what it is you want children to do, not what you do not want them to do.

- Sequence directions using "When-then." For example, "When things are put away where they belong, then we can go outside."

- Stay close. Merely standing near children can be enough to help them manage behavior. Be aware, however, that if you are talking to another adult, children may act out because they know they do not have your attention.

- Offer sufficient and appropriate choices. Children need a variety of activities that interest them and that will create opportunities for success.

## GETTING STARTED

There is always an array of information to learn when starting in a new position working with children. Use this fill-in-the-blank section to customize this resource book to your specific environment.

**What are the school's or center's hours of operation?**

On school days: _____

_____

_____

On vacation days: _____

_____

_____

**What is the basic daily schedule, and what are my responsibilities during each time segment?**

_____

_____

_____

_____

_____

_____

_____

**What are the procedures for checking children in and out of the program?**

_____

_____

_____

_____

**Do I call if I have to be absent? Who is my contact?**

Name: _____

Phone number: _____

**What is the dress code for employees?**

_____

_____

_____

**For what basic health and safety practices will I be responsible? Where are the materials stored for this (bleach, gloves, etc.)?**

Sanitizing tables: _____

_____

_____

Cleaning and maintaining equipment and materials: _____

_____

_____

_____

**What are the emergency procedures?**

Mildly injured child: _____

_____

_____

_____

Earthquake/tornado/hurricane: _____

_____

_____

Fire: _____

_____

_____

First aid: _____

_____

_____

Other: _____

_____

_____

_____

_____

_____

_____

_____

_____

_____

_____

_____

_____

_____

_____

# DEVELOPMENTAL MILESTONES BY AGE*

Whether you are working with infants, toddlers, preschoolers, or primary-aged children, a teacher's first requirement is to have knowledge about how children develop and learn. In your college program, you no doubt studied child development. The following is a shortened version of the universal steps most children go through as they develop. Some children will move easily from one step to another, whereas other children will move forward in one area but lag behind in others. Use these milestones as a guide for arranging an environment or planning activities in your room.

## BY SIX MONTHS OF AGE

Child's name: _____ Age: _____

Observer: _____ Date: _____

| | Yes | No | Sometimes |
|---|---|---|---|
| *Does the child . . .* | | | |
| show continued gains in height, weight, and head circumference? | | | |
| reach for toys or objects when they are presented? | | | |
| begin to roll from stomach to back? | | | |
| sit with minimal support? | | | |
| transfer objects from one hand to the other? | | | |
| raise up on arms, lifting head and chest, when placed on stomach? | | | |
| babble, coo, and imitate sounds? | | | |
| turn to locate the source of a sound? | | | |
| focus on an object and follow its movement vertically and horizontally? | | | |
| exhibit a blink reflex? | | | |
| enjoy being held and cuddled? | | | |
| recognize and respond to familiar faces? | | | |
| begin sleeping 6 to 8 hours through the night? | | | |
| suck vigorously when it is time to eat? | | | |
| enjoy playing in water during bath time? | | | |

*Some content in this section adapted from Allen, E. A., & Marotz, L. (2002). *Developmental profiles: Prebirth through twelve* (4th ed.). Clifton Park, NY: Thomson Delmar Learning.

## Developmental Alerts—One Month of Age

Check with a health care provider or early childhood specialist if, by *one month* of age, the infant *does not:*

- show alarm or "startle" responses to loud noise.

- suck and swallow with ease.

- show gains in height, weight, and head circumference.

- grasp with equal strength with both hands.

- make eye-to-eye contact when awake and being held.

- become quiet soon after being picked up.

- roll head from side to side when placed on stomach.

- express needs and emotions with cries and patterns of vocalizations that can be distinguished from one another.

- stop crying when picked up and held.

## Developmental Alerts—Four Months of Age

Check with a health care provider or early childhood specialist if, by *four months* of age, the infant *does not:*

- continue to show steady increases in height, weight, and head circumference.

- smile in response to the smiles of others (the social smile is a significant developmental milestone).

- follow a moving object with eyes focusing together.

- bring hands together over midchest.

- turn head to locate sounds.

- begin to raise head and upper body when placed on stomach.

- reach for objects or familiar persons.

## BY 12 MONTHS OF AGE

Child's name: _____ Age: _____

Observer: _____ Date: _____

| Does the child . . . | Yes | No | Sometimes |
|---|---|---|---|
| walk with assistance? | | | |
| roll a ball in imitation of an adult? | | | |
| pick objects up with thumb and forefinger? | | | |
| transfer objects from one hand to the other? | | | |
| pick up dropped toys? | | | |
| look directly at adult's face? | | | |
| imitate gestures: Peek-a-boo, bye-bye, Pat-a-cake? | | | |
| find object hidden under a cup? | | | |
| feed self crackers (munching, not sucking on them)? | | | |
| hold cup with two hands; drink with assistance? | | | |
| smile spontaneously? | | | |
| pay attention to own name? | | | |
| respond to "no"? | | | |
| respond differently to strangers and familiar persons? | | | |
| respond differently to sounds: vacuum, phone, door? | | | |
| look at person who speaks to him or her? | | | |
| respond to simple directions accompanied by gestures? | | | |
| make several consonant-vowel combination sounds? | | | |
| vocalize back to person who has talked to him or her? | | | |
| use intonation patterns that sound like scolding, asking, exclaiming? | | | |
| say "da-da" or "ma-ma"? | | | |

### Developmental Alerts

Check with a health care provider or early childhood specialist if, by *12 months* of age, the infant *does not:*

- blink when fast-moving objects approach the eyes.

- begin to cut teeth.

- imitate simple sounds.

- follow simple verbal requests: *come, bye-bye.*

- pull self to a standing position.

## BY TWO YEARS OF AGE

Child's name: _____ Age: _____

Observer: _____ Date: _____

| | Yes | No | Sometimes |
|---|---|---|---|
| *Does the child . . .* | | | |
| walk alone? | | | |
| bend over and pick up toy without falling over? | | | |
| seat self in child-size chair? | | | |
| walk up and down stairs with assistance? | | | |
| place several rings on a stick? | | | |
| place five pegs in a pegboard? | | | |
| turn pages two or three at a time? | | | |
| scribble? | | | |
| follow one-step direction involving something familiar? For example, "Give me _____." "Show me _____." "Get a_____." | | | |
| match familiar objects? | | | |
| use spoon with some spilling? | | | |
| hold cup with one hand and drink from it without assistance? | | | |
| chew food? | | | |
| take off coat, shoe, sock? | | | |
| zip and unzip large zipper? | | | |
| recognize self in mirror or picture? | | | |
| refer to self by name? | | | |
| imitate adult behaviors in play? For example, feeds "baby." | | | |
| help put things away? | | | |
| respond to specific words by showing what was named? For example, toy, pet, family member. | | | |
| ask for desired items by name? For example, cookie. | | | |
| answer with name of object when asked, "What's that?" | | | |
| make some two-word statements? For example, "Daddy bye-bye." | | | |

### Developmental Alerts

Check with a health care provider or early childhood specialist if, by *two years* of age, the child *does not*:

- attempt to talk or repeat words.
- understand some new words.

- respond to simple questions with "yes" or "no."
- walk alone (or with very little help).
- exhibit a variety of emotions: anger, delight, fear.
- show interest in pictures.
- recognize self in mirror.
- attempt self-feeding: hold own cup to mouth and drink.

## BY THREE YEARS OF AGE

Child's name: _____ Age: _____

Observer: _____ Date: _____

| | Yes | No | Sometimes |
|---|---|---|---|
| *Does the child . . .* | | | |
| run well in a forward direction? | | | |
| jump in place, with two feet together? | | | |
| walk on tiptoe? | | | |
| throw ball (but without direction or aim)? | | | |
| kick ball forward? | | | |
| string four large beads? | | | |
| turn pages in book singly? | | | |
| hold crayon: imitate circular, vertical, horizontal strokes? | | | |
| match shapes? | | | |
| demonstrate number concepts of 1 and 2? For example, can select 1 or 2; can tell if one or two objects. | | | |
| use spoon without spilling? | | | |
| drink from a straw? | | | |
| put on and take off coat? | | | |
| wash and dry hands with some assistance? | | | |
| watch other children; play near them; sometimes join in their play? | | | |
| defend own possessions? | | | |
| use symbols in play? For example, tin pan on head becomes helmet and crate becomes a spaceship. | | | |
| respond to "Put _____ in the box," "Take the _____ out of the box"? | | | |

|  | Yes | No | Sometimes |
|---|---|---|---|
| *Does the child . . .* |  |  |  |
| select correct item on request? For example, big versus little; one versus two. |  |  |  |
| identify objects by their use? For example, show own shoe when asked, "What do you wear on your feet?" |  |  |  |
| ask questions? |  |  |  |
| tell about something with functional phrases that carry meaning? For example, "Daddy go airplane," "Me hungry now." |  |  |  |

## Developmental Alerts

Check with a health care provider or early childhood specialist if, by *three years* of age, the child *does not*:

- eat a fairly well-rounded diet, even though amounts are limited.

- walk confidently, with few stumbles or falls; climb steps with help.

- avoid bumping into objects.

- follow simple, two-step directions ("Come to Daddy and bring your book"), express desires, ask questions.

- point to and name familiar objects; use two- or three-word sentences.

- enjoy being read to.

- show interest in playing with other children: watching, perhaps imitating.

- indicate a beginning interest in toilet training.

- sort familiar objects according to a single characteristic, such as type, color, or size.

## BY FOUR YEARS OF AGE

Child's name: _____ Age: _____

Observer: _____ Date: _____

|  | Yes | No | Sometimes |
|---|---|---|---|
| *Does the child . . .* | | | |
| walk on a line? | | | |
| balance on one foot briefly? Hop on one foot? | | | |
| jump over an object 6 inches high and land on both feet together? | | | |
| throw ball with direction? | | | |
| copy circles and X's? | | | |
| match six colors? | | | |
| count to 5? | | | |
| pour well from pitcher? Spread butter, jam with knife? | | | |
| button, unbutton large buttons? | | | |
| know own sex, age, last name? | | | |
| use toilet independently and reliably? | | | |
| wash and dry hands unassisted? | | | |
| listen to stories for at least 5 minutes? | | | |
| draw head of person and at least one other body part? | | | |
| play with other children? | | | |
| share, take turns (with some assistance)? | | | |
| engage in dramatic and pretend play? | | | |
| respond appropriately to "Put it beside," "Put it under"? | | | |
| respond to two-step directions? For example, "Give me the sweater and put the shoe on the floor." | | | |
| respond by selecting the correct object? For example, hard versus soft object. | | | |
| answer "if," "what," and "when" questions? | | | |
| answer questions about function? For example, "What are books for?" | | | |

**Developmental Alerts**

Check with a health care provider or early childhood specialist if, by *four years* of age, the child *does not:*

- have intelligible speech most of the time. (Have the child's hearing checked if there is any reason for concern.)

- understand and follow simple commands and directions.

- state own name and age.

- enjoy playing near or with other children.

- use three- to four-word sentences.

- ask questions.

- stay with an activity for 3 or 4 minutes; play alone several minutes at a time.

- jump in place without falling.

- balance on one foot, at least briefly.

- help with dressing self.

## FIVE TO SEVEN YEARS OF AGE

**Developmental Achievements**

- More independent of parents; able to take care of their own physical needs

- Rely upon their peer group for self-esteem; have two or three best friends

- Learn to share and take turns; participate in group games

- Are eager to learn and succeed in school

- Have a sense of duty and develop a conscience

- Are less aggressive and resolve conflicts with words

- Begin to see others' points of view

- Can sustain interest for long periods of time

- Can remember and relate past events

- Have good muscle control and can manage simple tools

- Have a high energy level

## BY FIVE YEARS OF AGE

Child's name: _____ Age: _____

Observer: _____ Date: _____

| | Yes | No | Sometimes |
|---|---|---|---|
| *Does the child . . .* | | | |
| walk backward, heel to toe? | | | |
| walk up and down stairs, alternating feet? | | | |
| cut on line? | | | |
| print some letters? | | | |
| point to and name three shapes? | | | |
| group common related objects? For example, shoe, sock, and foot; apple, orange, and plum. | | | |
| demonstrate number concepts to 4 or 5? | | | |
| cut food (for example, celery, sandwich) with a knife? | | | |
| lace shoes? | | | |
| read from story picture book? (In other words, does the child tell the story by looking at the pictures?) | | | |
| draw a person with three to six body parts? | | | |
| play and interact with other children; engage in dramatic play that is close to reality? | | | |
| build complex structures with blocks or other building materials? | | | |
| respond to simple three-step directions? For example, "Give me the pencil, put the book on the table, and hold the comb in your hand." | | | |
| respond correctly when asked to show a penny, nickel, and dime? | | | |
| ask "how" questions? | | | |
| respond verbally to "Hi" and "How are you?" | | | |
| tell about event using past and future tenses? | | | |
| use conjunctions to string words and phrases together? For example, "I saw a bear and a zebra and a giraffe at the zoo." | | | |

### Developmental Alerts

Check with a health care provider or early childhood specialist if, by *five years* of age, the child *does not:*

- state own name in full.

- recognize simple shapes: circle, square, triangle.

- catch a large ball when bounced. (Have the child's vision checked if there is any reason for concern.)

- speak so as to be understood by strangers. (Have the child's hearing checked if there is any reason for concern.)

- have good control of posture and movement.

- hop on one foot.

- appear interested in, and responsive to, surroundings.

- respond to statements without constantly asking to have them repeated.

- dress self with minimal adult assistance; manage buttons, zippers.

- take care of own toilet needs; have good bowel and bladder control with infrequent accidents.

## BY SIX YEARS OF AGE

Child's name: _____ Age: _____

Observer: _____ Date: _____

|  | Yes | No | Sometimes |
|---|---|---|---|
| *Does the child . . .* | | | |
| walk across a balance beam? | | | |
| skip with alternating feet? | | | |
| hop for several seconds on one foot? | | | |
| cut out simple shapes? | | | |
| copy own first name? | | | |
| show well-established handedness; demonstrate consistent right- or left-handedness? | | | |
| sort objects on one or more dimensions? For example, color, shape, or function. | | | |
| name most letters and numerals? | | | |
| count by rote to 10; know what number comes next? | | | |
| dress self completely; tie bows? | | | |
| brush teeth unassisted? | | | |
| have some concept of clock time in relation to daily schedule? | | | |
| cross street safely? | | | |

|  | Yes | No | Sometimes |
|---|---|---|---|
| *Does the child . . .* | | | |
| draw a person with head, trunk, legs, arms, and features; often add clothing details? | | | |
| play simple board games? | | | |
| engage in cooperative play with other children, involving group decisions, role assignments, rule observance? | | | |
| use construction toys, such as Legos® or blocks, to make recognizable structures? | | | |
| complete 15-piece puzzles? | | | |
| use all grammatical structures? For example, pronouns, plurals, verb tenses, conjunctions? | | | |
| use complex sentences? That is, the child can carry on conversations. | | | |

### Developmental Alerts

Check with a health care provider or early childhood specialist if, by *six years* of age, the child *does not*:

- alternate feet when walking up and down stairs.

- speak in a moderate voice; neither too loud or too soft nor too high or too low.

- follow simple directions in stated order: "Please go to the cupboard, get a cup, and bring it to me."

- use four to five words in an acceptable sentence structure.

- cut on a line with scissors.

- sit still and listen to an entire short story (5 to 7 minutes).

- maintain eye contact when spoken to (unless this is a cultural taboo).

- play well with other children.

- perform most self-grooming tasks independently: brush teeth, wash hands and face.

## BY SEVEN YEARS OF AGE

Child's name: _____ Age: _____

Observer: _____ Date: _____

| Does the child . . . | Yes | No | Sometimes |
|---|---|---|---|
| concentrate on completing puzzles and board games? | | | |
| ask many questions? | | | |
| use correct verb tenses, word order, and sentence structure in conversation? | | | |
| correctly identify right and left hands? | | | |
| make friends easily? | | | |
| show some control of anger, using words instead of physical aggression? | | | |
| participate in play that requires teamwork and rule observance? | | | |
| seek adult approval for efforts? | | | |
| enjoy reading and being read to? | | | |
| use a pencil to write words and numbers? | | | |
| sleep undisturbed through the night? | | | |
| catch a tennis ball, walk across a balance beam, hit a ball with a bat? | | | |
| plan and carry out simple projects with minimal adult help? | | | |
| tie own shoes? | | | |
| draw pictures with greater detail and sense of proportion? | | | |
| care for own personal needs with some adult supervision? For example, washes hands, brushes teeth, uses toilet, dresses self. | | | |
| show some understanding of cause-and-effect concepts? | | | |

### Developmental Alerts

Check with a health care provider or early childhood specialist if, by *seven years* of age, the child *does not:*

- show signs of ongoing growth: increasing height and weight; continuing motor development, such as running, jumping, balancing.

- show some interest in reading and trying to reproduce letters, especially those in own name.

- follow simple, multistep directions: "Finish your book, put it on the shelf, put your shoes on, and then get your coat on."

- follow through with instructions and complete simple tasks: putting dishes in the sink, picking up clothes, finishing a puzzle. *Note:* All children forget. Task incompletion is not a problem unless a child *repeatedly* leaves tasks unfinished.

- begin to develop alternatives to excessive use of inappropriate behaviors in order to get own way.

- develop a steady decrease in tension-type behaviors that may have developed with starting school: repeated grimacing or facial tics, eye twitching, grinding of teeth, regressive soiling or wetting, frequent stomachaches, refusing to go to school.

## EIGHT TO NINE YEARS OF AGE

### Developmental Achievements

- Need parental guidance and support for school achievement

- Are often competitive

- Have pronounced differences in interests by gender; same-gender cliques formed

- Spend a lot of time in physical game playing

- Consider academic achievement important

- Begin to develop moral values, make value judgments about own behavior

- Are aware of the importance of belonging

- Conform to gender roles

- Begin to think logically and to understand cause and effect

- Use language to communicate ideas and can use abstract words

- Can read but ability varies

- Realize importance of physical skills in determining status among peers

## BY EIGHT AND NINE YEARS OF AGE

Child's name: _____ Age: _____

Observer: _____ Date: _____

| | Yes | No | Sometimes |
|---|---|---|---|
| *Does the child . . .* | | | |
| have energy to play, continuing growth, few illnesses? | | | |
| use a pencil in a deliberate and controlled manner? | | | |
| express relatively complex thoughts in a clear and logical fashion? | | | |
| follow multiple four- to five-step instructions? | | | |
| become less easily frustrated with own performance? | | | |
| interact and play cooperatively with other children? | | | |
| show interest in creative expression? For example, tells stories and jokes, writes, draws, sings. | | | |
| use eating utensils with ease? | | | |
| have a good appetite; show interest in trying new foods? | | | |
| know how to tell time? | | | |
| have control of bowel and bladder functions? | | | |
| participate in some group activities? For example, games, sports, plays. | | | |
| want to go to school? Seem disappointed if must miss a day? | | | |
| demonstrate beginning skills in reading, writing, and math? | | | |
| accept responsibility and complete work independently? | | | |
| handle stressful situations without becoming overly upset? | | | |

### Developmental Alerts—Eight Years of Age

Check with a health care provider or early childhood specialist if, by *eight years* of age, the child *does not*:

- attend to the task at hand; show longer periods of sitting quietly, listening, responding appropriately.

- follow through on simple instructions.

- go to school willingly most days. (Of concern are excessive complaints about stomachaches or headaches when getting ready for school.)

- make friends. (Observe closely to see if the child plays alone most of the time or withdraws consistently from contact with other children.)

- sleep soundly most nights. (Frequent and recurring nightmares or bad dreams are usually at a minimum at this age.)

- seem to see or hear adequately at times (squints, rubs eyes excessively, asks frequently to have things repeated). (Have the child's vision and/or hearing checked if there is any reason for concern.)

- handle stressful situations without undue emotional upset (excessive crying, sleeping or eating disturbances, withdrawal, frequent anxiety).

- assume responsibility for personal care (dressing, bathing, feeding self) most of the time.

- show improved motor skills.

### Developmental Alerts—Nine Years of Age

Check with a health care provider or early childhood specialist if, by *nine years* of age, the child *does not:*

- exhibit a good appetite and continued weight gain. (Some children, especially girls, may already begin to show early signs of an eating disorder.)

- experience fewer illnesses.

- show improved motor skills, in terms of agility, speed, and balance.

- understand abstract concepts and use complex thought processes to problem solve.

- enjoy school and the challenge of learning.

- follow through on multistep instructions.

- express ideas clearly and fluently.

- form friendships with other children and enjoy participating in group activities.

## 10 TO 11 YEARS OF AGE

### Developmental Achievements

- Are less influenced by parents; may rebel

- Give importance to peer group, which sets standards for behavior

- Worry about what others think

- Choose friends based on common interests

- Have interests that differ based on gender

- Develop awareness and interest in opposite gender

- Begin to question adult authority

- Are often reluctant to attend child care; are bored or think they can care for themselves

- May be moody and experience stress over physical changes of puberty

- May be rebellious as they seek their own identity

- Can think abstractly and apply logic to solving problems

- Have a good command of spoken and written language

- Develop gender characteristics if female; begin a growth spurt if male

- May mature early, which is related to a positive self-image

- Are able to master physical skills necessary for playing games

## BY 10 AND 11 YEARS OF AGE

Child's name: _____ Age: _____

Observer: _____ Date: _____

| | Yes | No | Sometimes |
|---|---|---|---|
| *Does the child . . .* | | | |
| continue to increase in height and weight? | | | |
| exhibit improving coordination? For example, in running, climbing, riding a bike, writing. | | | |
| handle stressful situations without becoming overly upset or violent? | | | |
| construct sentences using reasonably correct grammar? For example, nouns, adverbs, verbs, adjectives. | | | |
| understand concepts of time, distance, space, volume? | | | |
| have one or two "best friends"? | | | |
| maintain friendships over time? | | | |

| | Yes | No | Sometimes |
|---|---|---|---|
| *Does the child . . .* | | | |
| approach challenges with a reasonable degree of self-confidence? | | | |
| play cooperatively and follow group instructions? | | | |
| begin to show an understanding of moral standards? For example, right from wrong, fairness, honesty, good from bad. | | | |
| look forward to, and enjoy, school? | | | |
| appear to hear well and listen attentively? | | | |
| enjoy reasonably good health, with few episodes of illness or health-related complaints? | | | |
| have a good appetite and enjoy mealtimes? | | | |
| take care of own personal hygiene without assistance? | | | |
| sleep through the night, waking up refreshed and energetic? | | | |

### Developmental Alerts

Check with a health care provider or early childhood specialist if, by *11 years* of age, the child *does not:*

- continue to grow at a rate appropriate for the child's gender.

- show continued improvement of fine motor skills.

- make or keep friends.

- enjoy going to school and show interest in learning. (Have children's hearing and vision tested; vision and hearing problems affect children's ability to learn and their interest in learning.)

- approach new situations with reasonable confidence.

- handle failure and frustration in a constructive manner.

- sleep through the night. Also check with a health care provider or early childhood specialist if the child experiences prolonged problems with bedwetting, nightmares, or sleepwalking.

## BY 12 AND 13 YEARS OF AGE

Child's name: _____ Age: _____

Observer: _____ Date: _____

| Does the child . . . | Yes | No | Sometimes |
|---|---|---|---|
| appear to be growing? For example, increasing height and maintaining a healthy weight (not too thin or too heavy). | | | |
| understand changes associated with puberty or have an opportunity to learn and ask questions? | | | |
| complain of headaches or blurred vision? | | | |
| have an abnormal posture or curving of the spine? | | | |
| seem energetic and not chronically fatigued? | | | |
| stay focused on a task and complete assignments? | | | |
| remember and carry out complex instructions? | | | |
| sequence, order, and classify objects? | | | |
| use longer and more complex sentence structure? | | | |
| engage in conversation; tell jokes and riddles? | | | |
| enjoy playing organized games and team sports? | | | |
| respond to anger-invoking situations without resorting to violence or physical aggression? | | | |
| begin to understand and solve complex mathematical problems? | | | |
| accept blame for actions on most occasions? | | | |
| enjoy competition? | | | |
| accept and carry out responsibility in a dependable manner? | | | |
| go to bed willingly and wake up refreshed? | | | |
| take pride in appearance; keep self reasonably clean? | | | |

### Developmental Alerts

Check with a health care provider or early childhood specialist if, by 13 years of age, the child does not:

- have movements that are smooth and coordinated.
- have energy sufficient for playing, riding bikes, or engaging in other desired activities.
- stay focused on tasks at hand.

- understand basic cause-and-effect relationships.

- handle criticism and frustration with a reasonable response. (Physical aggression and excessive crying could be an indication of other, underlying problems.)

- exhibit a healthy appetite. (Frequent skipping of meals is not typical for this age group.)

- make and keep friends.

As with the list of milestones by age, this list is not exhaustive, but it can be used to arrange an environment or to plan activities in your room.

## BIRTH TO ONE MONTH

| Physical | Date Observed |
|---|---|
| engages in primarily reflexive motor activity | |
| maintains "fetal" position, especially when sleeping | |
| holds hands in a fist; does not reach for objects | |
| in prone position, head falls lower than the body's horizontal line with hips flexed and arms and legs hanging down | |
| has good upper body muscle tone when supported under the arms | |
| **Cognitive** | |
| blinks in response to fast-approaching object | |
| follows a slowly moving object through a complete 180-degree arc | |
| follows objects moved vertically if close to face | |
| continues looking about, even in the dark | |
| begins to study own hand when lying in tonic neck reflex position | |
| prefers to listen to mother's voice rather than a stranger's | |
| **Language** | |
| cries and fusses as major forms of communication | |
| reacts to loud noises by blinking, moving (or stopping), shifting eyes, making a startle response | |
| shows preference for certain sounds (music and human voices) by calming down or quieting | |
| turns head to locate voices and other sounds | |
| makes occasional sounds other than crying | |

---

*Some content in this section adapted from Allen, E. A., & Marotz, L. (2002). *Developmental profiles: Prebirth through twelve* (4th ed.). Clifton Park, NY: Thomson Delmar Learning. Developmental milestones in Literacy sections adapted from Burns, S. M., Griffin, P., & Snow, C. E. (Eds.). (1999). *Starting out right: A guide to promoting children's reading success*. Washington, DC: National Academy Press.

| Social/Emotional | Date Observed |
|---|---|
| experiences a short period of alertness immediately following birth | |
| sleeps 17 to 19 hours a day; is gradually awake and responsive for longer periods | |
| likes to be held close and cuddled when awake | |
| shows qualities of individuality in responding or not responding to similar situations | |
| begins to establish emotional attachment or bonding with parents and caregivers | |
| begins to develop a sense of security/trust with parents and caregivers; responses to different individuals vary | |
| **Literacy** | |
| makes vocalizations in crib and while playing | |
| enjoys rhyming and other nonsense word play | |
| recognizes favorite book | |
| recognizes that pictures symbolize real objects | |
| does pretend reading of books | |
| enjoys listening to stories | |
| makes comments about pictures and characters in book | |
| labels objects in book | |
| asks adults to read or write with them | |
| transitions toward more purposeful scribbling | |
| can make some recognizable letterlike forms in scribbling | |
| combines drawing and writing | |
| becomes more careful with books and begins to understand their purpose | |

## ONE TO FOUR MONTHS

| Physical | Date Observed |
|---|---|
| has well-developed rooting and sucking reflexes | |
| in prone position, Landau reflex appears and baby raises head and upper body on arms | |
| grasps with entire hand; strength insufficient to hold items | |
| uses mostly large and jerky movements | |
| turns head side to side when in a supine (faceup) position | |
| begins rolling from front to back by turning head to one side and allowing trunk to follow | |
| **Cognitive** | |
| fixes on a moving object held at 12 inches (30.5 cm) | |
| continues to gaze in direction of moving objects that have disappeared | |

| Cognitive, continued | Date Observed |
|---|---|
| exhibits some sense of size/color/shape recognition of objects in the immediate environment | |
| alternates looking at an object, at one or both hands, and then back at the object | |
| moves eyes from one object to another | |
| focuses on small object and reaches for it; usually follows own hand movements | |
| **Language** | |
| reacts to sounds (voice, rattle, doorbell); later will search for source by turning head | |
| coordinates vocalization, looking, and body movements in face-to-face exchanges with parent or caregiver | |
| babbles or coos when spoken to or smiled at | |
| imitates own sounds and vowel sounds produced by others | |
| laughs out loud | |
| **Social/Emotional** | |
| imitates, maintains, terminates, and avoids interactions | |
| reacts differently to variations in adult voices | |
| enjoys being held and cuddled at times other than feeding and bedtime | |
| coos, gurgles, and squeals when awake | |
| smiles in response to a friendly face or voice | |
| entertains self for brief periods by playing with fingers, hands, and toes | |
| **Literacy** | |
| makes vocalizations in crib and while playing | |
| enjoys rhyming and other nonsense word play | |
| recognizes favorite book | |
| recognizes that pictures symbolize real objects | |
| does pretend reading of books | |
| enjoys listening to stories | |
| makes comments about pictures and characters in book | |
| labels objects in book | |
| asks adults to read or write with him or her | |
| transitions toward more purposeful scribbling | |
| can make some recognizable letterlike forms in scribbling | |
| combines drawing and writing | |
| becomes more careful with books and begins to understand their purpose | |

## FOUR TO EIGHT MONTHS

| Physical | Date Observed |
|---|---|
| shows signs of parachute reflex toward the end of this stage; exhibits swallowing reflex | |
| uses finger and thumb (pincer grip) to pick up objects | |
| reaches for objects with both arms simultaneously; later reaches with one hand | |
| transfers objects from one hand to the other; grasps object using palmar grasp | |
| handles, shakes, and pounds objects; puts everything in mouth | |
| sits alone without support (holds head erect, back straight, arms propped forward for support) | |
| **Cognitive** | |
| turns toward and locates familiar voices and sounds | |
| uses hand, mouth, and eyes in coordination to explore own body, toys, and surroundings | |
| imitates actions, such as Pat-a-cake, bye-bye, and Peek-a-boo | |
| shows fear of falling from high places, such as changing table, stairs | |
| looks over side of crib or high chair for objects dropped; delights in repeatedly throwing objects overboard for adult to retrieve | |
| bangs objects together playfully; bangs spoon or toy on table | |
| **Language** | |
| responds appropriately to own name and simple requests, such as "Eat," "Wave bye-bye" | |
| imitates some nonspeech sounds, such as coughing, tongue clicking, lip smacking | |
| produces a full range of vowels and some consonants: r, s, z, th, and w | |
| responds to variations in the tone of voice of others | |
| expresses emotions (pleasure, satisfaction, anger) by making different sounds | |
| babbles by repeating same syllable in a series: ba, ba, ba | |
| **Social/Emotional** | |
| delights in observing surroundings; continuously watches people and activities | |
| begins to develop an awareness of self as a separate individual from others | |
| becomes more outgoing and social in nature: smiles, coos, reaches out | |
| distinguishes among, and responds differently to, strangers, teachers, parents, siblings | |
| responds differently and appropriately to facial expressions: frowns; smiles | |
| imitates facial expressions, actions, and sounds | |

| Literacy | Date Observed |
|---|---|
| makes vocalizations in crib and while playing | |
| enjoys rhyming and other nonsense word play | |
| recognizes favorite book | |
| recognizes that pictures symbolize real objects | |
| does pretend reading of books | |
| enjoys listening to stories | |
| makes comments about pictures and characters in book | |
| labels objects in book | |
| asks adults to read or write with him or her | |
| transitions toward more purposeful scribbling | |
| can make some recognizable letterlike forms in scribbling | |
| combines drawing and writing | |
| becomes more careful with books and begins to understand their purpose | |

## EIGHT TO TWELVE MONTHS

| Physical | Date Observed |
|---|---|
| reaches with one hand leading to grasp an offered object or toy | |
| manipulates objects, transferring them from one hand to the other | |
| explores new objects by poking with one finger | |
| uses deliberate pincer grip to pick up small objects, toys, and finger foods | |
| stacks objects; also places objects inside one another | |
| releases objects by dropping or throwing; cannot intentionally put an object down | |
| begins pulling self to a standing position; begins to stand alone | |
| **Cognitive** | |
| watches people, objects, and activities in the immediate environment | |
| shows awareness of distant objects (15 to 20 feet away) by pointing at them | |
| reaches for toys that are visible but out of reach | |
| continues to drop first item when other toys or items are offered | |
| recognizes the reversal of an object: cup upside down is still a cup | |
| imitates activities: hitting two blocks together, playing Pat-a-cake | |
| **Language** | |
| babbles or jabbers to initiate social interaction; may shout to attract attention | |
| shakes head for "no" and may nod for "yes" | |
| responds by looking for voice when name is called | |

| Language, continued | Date Observed |
|---|---|
| babbles in sentence-like sequences; followed by jargon (syllables/sounds with language-like inflection) | |
| waves "bye-bye"; claps hands when asked | |
| says "da-da" and "ma-ma" | |
| **Social/Emotional** | |
| exhibits a definite fear of strangers; clings to, or hides behind, parent or caregiver ("stranger anxiety"); resists separating from familiar adult ("separation anxiety") | |
| enjoys being near, and included in, daily activities of family members and teachers; is becoming more sociable and outgoing | |
| enjoys novel experiences and opportunities to examine new objects | |
| shows need to be picked up and held by extending arms upward, crying, or clinging to adult's legs | |
| begins to exhibit assertiveness by resisting caregiver's requests; may kick, scream, or throw self on the floor | |
| **Literacy** | |
| enjoys rhyming and other nonsense word play | |
| recognizes favorite book | |
| recognizes that pictures symbolize real objects | |
| does pretend reading of books | |
| enjoys listening to stories | |
| makes comments about pictures and characters in book | |
| labels objects in book | |
| asks adults to read or write with him or her | |
| transitions toward more purposeful scribbling | |
| can make some recognizable letterlike forms in scribbling | |
| combines drawing and writing | |
| becomes more careful with books and begins to understand their purpose | |

## ONE YEAR OF AGE

| Physical | Date Observed |
|---|---|
| crawls skillfully and quickly; gets to feet unaided | |
| stands alone with feet spread apart, legs stiffened, and arms extended for support | |
| walks unassisted near the end of this period (most children); falls often; not always able to maneuver around furniture or toys | |

| Physical, continued | Date Observed |
|---|---|
| uses furniture to lower self to floor; collapses backward into a sitting position or falls forward on hands and then sits | |
| releases an object voluntarily | |
| enjoys pushing or pulling toys while walking | |
| **Cognitive** | |
| enjoys object-hiding activities: early on, will search same location for a hidden object; later will search in several locations | |
| passes toy to other hand when offered a second object ("crossing the midline") | |
| manages three to four objects by setting an object aside (on lap or floor) when presented with a new toy | |
| puts toys in mouth less often | |
| enjoys looking at picture books | |
| demonstrates understanding of functional relationships (objects that belong together) | |
| **Language** | |
| produces considerable "jargon": combines words/sounds into speechlike patterns | |
| uses one word to convey an entire thought (holophrastic speech); later, produces two-word phrases to express a complete thought (telegraphic speech) | |
| follows simple directions: "Give Daddy the cup" | |
| points to familiar persons, animals, and toys when asked | |
| identifies three body parts if someone names them: "Show me your nose (toe, ear)" | |
| indicates a few desired objects/activities by name: "bye-bye," "cookie"; verbal request is often accompanied by an insistent gesture | |
| **Social/Emotional** | |
| remains friendly toward others; usually less wary of strangers | |
| helps pick up and put away toys | |
| plays alone for short periods and does not play cooperatively | |
| enjoys being held and read to | |
| imitates adult actions in play | |
| enjoys adult attention; likes to know that an adult is near; gives hugs and kisses | |
| **Literacy** | |
| enjoys rhyming and other nonsense word play | |
| recognizes favorite book | |
| recognizes that pictures symbolize real objects | |
| does pretend reading of books | |
| enjoys listening to stories | |
| makes comments about pictures and characters in book | |

| Literacy, continued | Date Observed |
|---|---|
| labels objects in book | |
| asks adults to read or write with him or her | |
| transitions toward more purposeful scribbling | |
| can make some recognizable letterlike forms in scribbling | |
| combines drawing and writing | |
| becomes more careful with books and begins to understand their purpose | |

## TWO YEARS OF AGE

| Physical | Date Observed |
|---|---|
| walks with a more erect, heel-to-toe pattern; can maneuver around obstacles in pathway | |
| runs with greater confidence; has fewer falls | |
| squats for long periods while playing | |
| climbs stairs unassisted (but not with alternating feet) | |
| balances on one foot (for a few moments), jumps up and down, but may fall | |
| begins to achieve toilet training (depending on physical and neurological development), although accidents should still be expected; will indicate readiness for toilet training | |
| **Cognitive** | |
| exhibits better coordinated eye-hand movements; can put objects together, take them apart; fit large pegs into pegboard | |
| begins to use objects for purposes other than intended (pushes block around as boat) | |
| completes classification based on one dimension (separates toy dinosaurs from toy cars) | |
| stares for long moments; seems fascinated by, or engrossed in, figuring out a situation | |
| attends to self-selected activities for longer periods of time | |
| shows discovery of cause and effect: squeezing the cat makes it scratch | |
| **Language** | |
| enjoys being read to if allowed to point, make relevant noises, turn pages | |
| realizes that language is effective for getting others to respond to needs and preferences | |
| uses 50 to 300 different words; vocabulary continuously increasing | |
| has broken linguistic code; in other words, much of a two-year-old's talk has meaning to him or her | |

| Language, continued | Date Observed |
|---|---|
| understands more language than can communicate verbally; most two-year-olds' receptive language is more developed than their expressive language | |
| utters three- and four-word statements; uses conventional word order to form more complete sentences | |
| **Social/Emotional** | |
| shows empathy and caring | |
| continues to use physical aggression if frustrated or angry (more exaggerated in some children); physical aggression lessens as verbal skills improve | |
| expresses frustration through temper tantrums; tantrum frequency peaks during this year; cannot be reasoned with while tantrum is in progress | |
| finds it difficult to wait or take turns; is often impatient | |
| enjoys "helping" with household chores; imitates everyday activities | |
| orders parents and teachers around; makes demands and expects immediate compliance | |
| **Literacy** | |
| enjoys rhyming and other nonsense word play | |
| recognizes favorite book | |
| recognizes that pictures symbolize real objects | |
| does pretend reading of books | |
| enjoys listening to stories | |
| makes comments about pictures and characters in book | |
| labels objects in book | |
| asks adults to read or write with him or her | |
| transitions toward more purposeful scribbling | |
| can make some recognizable letterlike forms in scribbling | |
| combines drawing and writing | |
| becomes more careful with books and begins to understand their purpose | |

## THREE YEARS OF AGE

| Physical | Date Observed |
|---|---|
| walks unassisted up and down stairs, alternating feet; may jump from bottom step, landing on both feet | |
| balances momentarily on one foot | |
| kicks a large ball, catches a large bounced ball with both arms extended | |
| feeds self; needs minimal assistance | |

| Physical, continued | Date Observed |
|---|---|
| jumps in place | |
| pedals a small tricycle or wheeled toy | |
| **Cognitive** | |
| listens attentively and makes relevant comments during age-appropriate stories, especially those related to home and family events | |
| likes to look at books and may pretend to "read" to others or explain pictures | |
| enjoys stories with riddles, guessing, and suspense | |
| points with fair accuracy to correct pictures when given sound-alike words: keys–cheese; fish–dish; mouse–mouth | |
| plays realistically: feeds doll; hooks truck and trailer together | |
| places eight to ten pegs in pegboard, or six round and six square blocks in form board | |
| **Language** | |
| talks about objects, events, and people not present: "Jerry has a pool in his yard" | |
| talks about the actions of others: "Daddy's mowing the grass" | |
| adds information to what has just been said: "Yeah, and then he grabbed it back" | |
| answers simple questions appropriately | |
| asks increasing numbers of questions, including location/identity of objects and people | |
| uses increased speech forms to keep conversation going: "What did he do next?" "How come she hid?" | |
| **Social/Emotional** | |
| seems to understand taking turns, but not always willing to do so | |
| laughs frequently; is friendly and eager to please | |
| has occasional nightmares and fears the dark, monsters, or fire | |
| joins in simple games and group activities, sometimes hesitantly | |
| talks to self often | |
| uses objects symbolically in play: block of wood may be a truck, a ramp, a bat | |
| **Literacy** | |
| realizes that alphabet letters are unique visuals and can be named | |
| recognizes many forms of print in the environment, such as product logos | |
| attends to the sounds at the beginning of words | |
| can participate in making rhyming words | |
| gives attention to repeated sounds in words | |
| understands that the words printed in books are read to make the story | |
| uses new vocabulary | |
| begins to use rudimentary grammatical structures with some accuracy | |

| Literacy, continued | Date Observed |
|---|---|
| can follow a short sequence of oral directions | |
| connects information read to real-life situations | |
| understands stories and concepts in a very literal and concrete way | |
| desires for others to observe his or her reading and writing attempts | |
| can identify most letters in own name | |
| can identify about 10 alphabet letters | |
| enjoys scribbling as a way to communicate with friends in dramatic play | |

## FOUR YEARS OF AGE

| Physical | Date Observed |
|---|---|
| walks a straight line (tape or chalk line on the floor) | |
| hops on one foot | |
| pedals and steers a wheeled toy with confidence; avoids obstacles and oncoming "traffic" | |
| climbs ladders, trees, playground equipment | |
| jumps over objects 5 or 6 inches (12.5 to 15 cm) high; lands with both feet together | |
| runs, starts, stops, and moves around obstacles with ease | |
| **Cognitive** | |
| stacks at least five graduated cubes largest to smallest; builds a pyramid of six blocks | |
| indicates if paired words sound the same or different: sheet–feet, ball–wall | |
| names 18 to 20 uppercase letters near the end of this year; may be able to print several and write own name; may recognize some printed words (especially those that have special meaning) | |
| may begin to read simple books (alphabet books with few words per page and many pictures) | |
| likes stories about how things grow and operate | |
| delights in word play, creating silly language | |
| **Language** | |
| uses the prepositions *on, in,* and *under* | |
| uses possessives consistently: hers, theirs, baby's | |
| answers "Whose?" "Who?" "Why?" and "How many?" | |
| produces elaborate sentence structures | |
| uses almost entirely intelligible speech | |

| Language, continued | Date Observed |
|---|---|
| begins to correctly use the past tense of verbs: "Mommy closed the door," "Daddy went to work" | |
| **Social/Emotional** | |
| is outgoing and friendly; overly enthusiastic at times | |
| changes moods rapidly and unpredictably; often throws tantrum over minor frustrations; sulks over being left out | |
| holds conversations and shares strong emotions with imaginary playmates or companions; invisible friends are common | |
| boasts, exaggerates, and "bends" the truth with made-up stories or claims; tests limits with "bathroom" talk | |
| cooperates with others; participates in group activities | |
| shows pride in accomplishments; seeks frequent adult approval | |
| **Literacy** | |
| realizes that alphabet letters are unique visuals and can be named | |
| recognizes many forms of print in the environment, such as product logos | |
| attends to the sounds at the beginning of words | |
| can participate in making rhyming words | |
| gives attention to repeated sounds in words | |
| understands that the words printed in books are read to make the story | |
| uses new vocabulary | |
| begins to use rudimentary grammatical structures with some accuracy | |
| can follow a short sequence of oral directions | |
| connects information read to real-life situations | |
| understands stories and concepts in a very literal and concrete way | |
| desires for others to observe his or her reading and writing attempts | |
| can identify most letters in own name | |
| can identify at least 10 alphabet letters | |
| enjoys scribbling as a way to communicate with friends in dramatic play | |

## FIVE YEARS OF AGE

| Physical | Date Observed |
|---|---|
| walks backward, heel to toe | |
| walks unassisted up and down stairs, alternating feet | |
| learns to turn somersaults (should be taught the right way in order to avoid injury) | |
| touches toes without flexing knees | |

| Physical, continued | Date Observed |
|---|---|
| catches a ball thrown from 3 feet away | |
| rides a tricycle or wheeled toy with speed and skillful steering; some learn to ride bicycles, usually with training wheels | |
| **Cognitive** | |
| forms rectangle from two triangular cuts | |
| builds steps with set of small blocks | |
| understands concept of same shape, same size | |
| sorts objects on the basis of two dimensions, such as color and form | |
| sorts objects so that all things in the group have a single common feature | |
| understands smallest and shortest; places objects in order from shortest to tallest, smallest to largest | |
| **Language** | |
| has vocabulary of 1,500 words or more | |
| tells a familiar story while looking at pictures in a book | |
| uses functional definitions: a ball is to bounce; a bed is to sleep in | |
| identifies and names four to eight colors | |
| recognizes the humor in simple jokes; makes up jokes and riddles | |
| produces sentences with five to seven words; much longer sentences are not unusual | |
| **Social/Emotional** | |
| enjoys friendships; often has one or two special playmates | |
| shares toys, takes turns, plays cooperatively (with occasional lapses); is often quite generous | |
| participates in play and activities with other children; suggests imaginative and elaborate play ideas | |
| is affectionate and caring, especially toward younger or injured children and animals | |
| follows directions and carries out assignments usually; generally does what parent or teacher requests | |
| continues to need adult comfort and reassurance, but may be less open in seeking and accepting comfort | |
| **Literacy** | |
| understands that books have different parts with different functions | |
| begins to informally track print and will recognize when parts are omitted | |
| will pretend read familiar stories | |
| can name and recognize all uppercase and lowercase letters | |
| can write most letters | |
| can write first and last name | |

| Literacy, continued | Date Observed |
|---|---|
| begins to understand conventional writing | |
| uses a combination of conventional and nonconventional spelling | |
| often uses letter sounds for nonconventional spelling | |
| understands that the sequence of letters in a word represents a sequence of sounds, which forms a word with meaning | |
| learns many letter-sound correspondences | |
| has increased use of vocabulary and grammatical skills | |
| can write many uppercase and lowercase letters | |
| can give rhymes for most words | |
| can identify words that begin with the same sound | |
| can blend or merge segments or syllables of words into meaningful words | |
| recognizes a few common sight words | |
| understands the differences in oral and written language | |
| enjoys reenacting and retelling stories | |
| listens attentively to stories read or told by others | |
| can names some of favorite authors and book titles | |
| begins to see differences in different types of print (for example, poems, signs, books) | |
| can answer questions about stories read to them | |
| can make predictions about what will happen in the story | |
| understands that phonemes are joined together in a particular sequence to make words | |

## SIX YEARS OF AGE

| Physical | Date Observed |
|---|---|
| has increased muscle strength; typically boys are stronger than girls of similar size | |
| gains greater control over large and fine motor skills; movements are more precise and deliberate, although some clumsiness persists | |
| enjoys vigorous physical activity: running, jumping, climbing, and throwing | |
| moves constantly, even when trying to sit still | |
| has increased dexterity, improved eye-hand coordination, and improved motor functioning, which facilitate learning to ride a bicycle, swim, swing a bat, or kick a ball | |
| enjoys art projects: likes to paint, model with clay, "make things," draw and color, work with wood | |

| Cognitive | |
|---|---|
| shows increased attention; works at tasks for longer periods, although concentrated effort is not always consistent | |
| understands simple time markers (today, tomorrow, yesterday) or uncomplicated concepts of motion (cars go faster than bicycles) | |
| recognizes seasons and major holidays and the activities associated with each | |
| enjoys puzzles, counting and sorting activities, paper-and-pencil mazes, and games that involve matching letters and words with pictures | |
| recognizes some words by sight; attempts to sound out words (some may read well by this time) | |
| identifies familiar coins: pennies, nickels, dimes, quarters | |
| **Language** | |
| loves to talk, often nonstop; may be described as a chatterbox | |
| carries on adultlike conversations; asks many questions | |
| learns 5 to 10 new words daily; vocabulary consists of 10,000 to 14,000 words | |
| uses appropriate verb tenses, word order, and sentence structure | |
| uses language (not tantrums or physical aggression) to express displeasure: "That's mine! Give it back, you dummy" | |
| talks self through steps required in simple problem-solving situations (although the "logic" may be unclear to adults) | |
| **Social/Emotional** | |
| experiences mood swings: "best friends" then "worst enemies"; loving then uncooperative and irritable; especially unpredictable toward mother or primary caregiver | |
| becomes less dependent on parents as friendship circle expands; still needs closeness and nurturing but has urges to break away and "grow up" | |
| needs and seeks adult approval, reassurance, and praise; may complain excessively about minor hurts to gain more attention | |
| continues to be egocentric; still sees events almost entirely from own perspective: views everything and everyone as there for his or her own benefit | |
| is easily disappointed and frustrated by self-perceived failure | |
| has difficulty composing and soothing self; cannot tolerate being corrected or losing at games; may sulk, cry, refuse to play, or reinvent rules to suit own purposes | |

## SEVEN YEARS OF AGE

| Physical | Date Observed |
|---|---|
| exhibits large and fine motor control that is more finely tuned | |
| tends to be cautious in undertaking more challenging physical activities, such as climbing up or jumping down from high places | |
| practices a new motor skill repeatedly until mastered, then moves on to something else | |
| finds floor more comfortable than furniture when reading or watching television; legs often in constant motion | |
| uses knife and fork appropriately but inconsistently | |
| tightly grasps pencil near the tip; rests head on forearm, lowers head almost to the tabletop when doing pencil-and-paper tasks | |

| Cognitive | |
|---|---|
| understands concepts of space and time in both logical and practical ways: a year is "a long time"; 100 miles is "far away" | |
| begins to grasp concepts of conservation, as defined by Piaget (for example, the shape of a container does not necessarily reflect what it can hold) | |
| gains a better understanding of cause and effect: "If I'm late for school again, I'll be in big trouble" | |
| tells time by the clock and understands calendar time—days, months, years, seasons | |
| plans ahead: "I'm saving this cookie for tonight" | |
| shows marked fascination with magic tricks; enjoys putting on "shows" for parents and friends | |

| Language | |
|---|---|
| enjoys storytelling; likes to write short stories, tell imaginative tales | |
| uses adultlike sentence structure and language in conversation; patterns reflect cultural and geographical differences | |
| becomes more precise and elaborate in use of language; greater use of descriptive adjectives and adverbs | |
| uses gestures to illustrate conversations | |
| criticizes own performance: "I didn't draw that right," "Her picture is better than mine" | |
| exaggerates verbally (common): "I ate 10 hot dogs at the picnic." | |

| Social/Emotional | |
|---|---|
| is cooperative and affectionate toward adults and less frequently annoyed with them; sees humor in everyday happenings | |
| likes to be the "teacher's helper"; eager for teacher's attention and approval but less obvious about seeking it | |

| Social/Emotional, continued | Date Observed |
|---|---|
| seeks out friendships; friends are important, but can stay busy if no one is available | |
| quarrels less often, although squabbles and tattling continue in both one-on-one and group play | |
| complains that family decisions are unjust, that a particular sibling gets to do more or is given more | |
| blames others for own mistakes; makes up alibis for personal shortcomings: "I could have made a better one, but my teacher didn't give me enough time" | |

## EIGHT YEARS OF AGE

| Physical | Date Observed |
|---|---|
| enjoys vigorous activity; likes to dance, roller blade, swim, wrestle, bicycle, fly kites | |
| seeks opportunities to participate in team activities and games: soccer, baseball, kickball | |
| exhibits significant improvement in agility, balance, speed, and strength | |
| copies words and numbers from blackboard with increasing speed and accuracy; has good eye-hand coordination | |
| possesses seemingly endless energy | |
| **Cognitive** | |
| collects objects; organizes and displays items according to more complex systems; bargains and trades with friends to obtain additional pieces | |
| saves money for small purchases; eagerly develops plans to earn cash for odd jobs; studies catalogues and magazines for items to purchase | |
| begins taking an interest in what others think and do; understands there are differences of opinion, cultures, distant countries | |
| accepts challenge and responsibility with enthusiasm; delights in being asked to perform tasks at home and in school; is interested in being rewarded | |
| likes to read and work independently; spends considerable time planning and making lists | |
| understands perspective (shadow, distance, shape); drawings reflect more realistic portrayal of objects | |
| **Language** | |
| delights in telling jokes and riddles | |
| understands and carries out multistep instructions (up to five steps); may need directions repeated because of not listening to the entire request | |
| enjoys writing letters or sending e-mail messages to friends; includes imaginative and detailed descriptions | |
| uses language to criticize and compliment others; repeats slang and curse words | |

| Language, continued | Date Observed |
|---|---|
| understands and follows rules of grammar in conversation and written form | |
| is intrigued with learning secret word codes and using code language | |
| converses fluently with adults; can think and talk about past and future: "What time are we leaving to get to the swim meet next week?" | |
| **Social/Emotional** | |
| begins forming opinions about moral values and attitudes; declares things right or wrong | |
| plays with two or three "best" friends, most often the same age and gender; also enjoys spending some time alone | |
| seems less critical of own performance but is easily frustrated when unable to complete a task or when the product does not meet expectations | |
| enjoys team games and activities; values group membership and acceptance by peers | |
| continues to blame others or makes up alibis to explain own shortcomings or mistakes | |
| enjoys talking on the telephone with friends | |

# PLAY MATERIALS FOR CHILDREN

Children construct their own understanding of the world around them as they interact with appropriate materials and with other people. Teachers play an important role in providing choices of good-quality playthings that match children's developmental abilities and interests. When budgets are limited, it is vital that teachers be able to select toys and materials that will provide optimal learning opportunities. Creative teachers learn how to "scrounge" for toys and how to make playthings out of recycled materials.

## FOR TODDLERS (ONE TO THREE YEARS)

### For Pretend Play

- small wood or plastic people and animal figures
- small cars and trucks
- dolls
- plastic dishes and pots and pans
- doll beds
- hats
- simple dress-ups
- telephones
- scarves and fabrics

## FOR CHILDREN AGES THREE THOUGH FIVE

### Exploration and Mastery Play Materials

- puzzles, including fit-in puzzles and large, simple jigsaw puzzles, with varying numbers of pieces, according to children's age

- pattern-making materials: beads for stringing, pegboards, mosaic boards, felt boards, color cubes

- beginning computer programs

- games: dominoes; lotto games; bingo by color, number, or picture; first board games that use concepts such as color or counting; Memory

- books of all kinds: picture books, realistic stories, alphabet picture books, poetry, information books

- writing center materials: clipboards, colored pencils, old calendars, envelopes, notepads, stationary, rubber stamps and ink pads, rulers, magnetic letters, stencil shapes, stickers, file cards, and office materials

### For Pretend Play

- dolls of various ethnic and gender appearance, with clothes and other accessories and furniture

- housekeeping equipment

- variety of dress-ups, including those related to various roles and themes

- transportation toys

- hand puppets

- animal and human figures for play scenes

- full-length, unbreakable mirror

### For Creative Play

- recorded music for singing, movement and dancing, and listening and for using with rhythm instruments

## FOR CHILDREN SIX THROUGH EIGHT YEARS

### For Exploration and Mastery Play*

- puzzles: 100-piece jigsaw puzzles, three-dimensional puzzles like Rubik's® cubes

- craft materials for braiding, weaving, knitting, leather craft, jewelry making, sewing

- pattern-making materials: mosaic tiles, geometric puzzles

- games: word games, simple card games, reading and spelling games, number and counting games, beginning strategy games such as checkers

- computer programs for language arts and for problem-solving activities

- books at a variety of levels for beginning readers—see the Additional Resource(s) list in the supplement

### For Creative Activities*

- music for singing and movement

- audiovisual materials for independent use

Remember that recycled materials and other loose parts have many uses for exploration and creativity. These materials can be valuable tools in a number of curriculum areas†:

- magazines with colorful pictures, which are excellent for making collages, murals, and posters

- scraps of fabric—felt, silk, cotton, oil cloth, and so forth, which can be used to make "fabric boards" with the name of each fabric written under a small swatch attached to the board, as well as for collages, puppets, and so on

If you are responsible for ordering supplies for your classroom or early childhood program, the following guidelines will be useful.

---

*Some ideas adapted from Bronson, M. (1995). *The right stuff for children birth to 8: Selecting play materials to support development.* Washington, DC: NAEYC.

†Adapted from Mayesky, M. (2002). *Creative activities for young children* (7th ed.). Clifton Park, NY: Thomson Delmar Learning.

## BASIC PROGRAM EQUIPMENT AND MATERIALS FOR AN EARLY CHILDHOOD CENTER

### Indoor Equipment

The early childhood room should be arranged into well-planned areas of interest, such as the housekeeping and doll corner, block building, and so forth, to encourage children to play in small groups throughout the playroom, engaging in activities of their special interest, rather than attempting to play in one large group.

The early childhood center must provide selections of indoor play equipment from many areas of interest. Selection should be of sufficient quantities so that children can participate in a wide range of activities. Many pieces of equipment can be homemade. Consider the age and developmental levels of the children when making selections.

### Playroom Furnishings

- Tables—seat four to six children (18″ high for three-year-olds, 20–22″ high for four- and five-year-olds)

- Chairs—10″ high for three-year-olds, 12–14″ high for four- and five-year-olds

- Open shelves—26″ high, 12″ deep, 12″ between shelves

- Lockers—12″ wide, 12″ deep, 32 to 36″ high

### Housekeeping or Doll Corner

| Item | Number Recommended for 10 Children |
| --- | --- |
| dolls | 3 |
| doll clothes | variety |
| doll bed—should be large enough for a child to get into and include bedding | 1 |
| doll high chair | 1 |
| small table, four chairs | 1 set |
| tea party dishes | 6-piece set with tray |
| stove—child size, approximately 24″ high, 23″ long, 12″ wide | 1 |

| Item | Number Recommended for 10 Children |
|---|---|
| sink—child size, approximately 24" high, 23" long, 12" wide | 1 |
| refrigerator—child size, approximately 28" high, 23" long, 12" wide | 1 |
| pots and pans, empty food cartons, measuring cups, spoons, etc. | variety |
| mop, broom, dustpan | 1 |
| ironing board and iron | 1 |
| clothespins and clothesline | 1 |
| toy telephones | 2 |
| dress-up box—men's and women's hats, neckties, pocketbooks, wallets, shoes, old dresses, scarves, jewelry, etc. | variety |
| mirror | 1 |

## Books and Stories (20–30 Books)

A carefully selected book collection for the various age levels should include the following:

- transportation, birds and animals, family life
- community helpers, science, nonsense rhymes
- Mother Goose rhymes, poems, and stories
- homemade picture books
- collection of pictures classified by subject
- library books to enrich the collection

# OBSERVATION AND ASSESSMENT

There are a variety of tools that can be used to assess children's development. Using assessment tools in conjunction with developmental milestones helps caregivers recognize a child's developmental accomplishments as well as determine the child's next growth steps. Not all children will give as much time to the teacher's directions. The teacher needs to observe each child to determine the level to which each child is performing independently so that instruction can begin. This knowledge is useful in planning curriculum, designing the room environment for success, and establishing appropriate techniques that help children manage their own behavior. No doubt your college practicum experience taught you the logistics of observing: using objective descriptions and recording specific, dated, brief, and factual information. Observation can take many forms:

- anecdotal records

- running records

- checklists

- time or event sampling

**Anecdotal records** are brief notes kept by the teacher while the child is performing a task. At first this may seem daunting, but it will become part of your everyday routine. Keep a small spiral notebook and pen or pencil in your pocket. When a child begins an activity, watch what the child does and write down three or four things that you actually observe the child doing. Remember the facts and only the facts.*

- Anecdotal notes are authored by the teacher for future use to assist learning outcomes and the understanding of children of which they work with.

*Adapted from Bentzen, W. R. (1996). *Seeing young children: A guide to observing and recording behavior* (5th ed.). Clifton Park, NY: Thomson Delmar Learning.

- Avoid opinions and assumptions.

- Record only what you observe.

- Remember to be prepared to record exactly what you see the child doing at the time it occurs to ensure accuracy.

- Be sure to include information concerning the setting and context of what is occurring because these affect a child's behavior.

- Record actual dialogue of conversation between the child and any individual.

- It is imperative to keep your inferences apart from the observed behavior. Also, note this information in your note taking and narratives as inferences or interpretations.

- Document in your note taking whether the observed behavior is typical or atypical of the child being observed during this time of observation.

As time permits, probably during nap time, the brief notes are turned into a full scenario so that anyone could read the record at a later date:

## ANECDOTAL RECORD

Child's name: **Johnny H.**                          Age: 7 yr. 5 mo.

Observer: Jorge                          Date: July 27, 2006

| What Actually Happened/What I Saw | Developmental Interpretation (Select 1 or 2 of the following) | |
|---|---|---|
| **Child Observed:** Jon | Interest in learning | X |
| **Observation Setting:** toddler classroom, during circle time | Self-esteem/self-concept | X |
| | Cultural acceptance | |
| **Observer:** Ms. Thinner, classroom teacher | Problem solving | |
| **Date:** 7/27/06 | Interest in real-life mathematical concepts | |
| **Description of Observed Child:** Jon is observed sitting with his legs out-stretched during circle time. Upon refusing | Interactions with adults | X |
| | Literacy | X |
| | Interactions with peers | |

| What Actually Happened/What I Saw | Developmental Interpretation (Select 1 or 2 of the following) | |
|---|---|---|
| to sit with his legs folded, he rocks while sitting and sucks on his pointer and index fingers. While refusing to join in on the groups activities, he is observed watching the groups' interaction. Both Ms. Tucker and Mr. Lee, the assistant teacher, eagerly encourage Jon to join the activities. "Jon, will you help me sing our morning song?" says his teacher. "No," whispers, Jon. The groups begins to sing as Ms. Tucker moves closer to Jon, placing her hand on his shoulder as she moves from child to child with a morning greeting. Jon quickly moves away to avoid being touched. As the group continues the morning activities of identifying the day, the month, and current weather conditions, Jon eagerly observes but refuses to participate himself. As Ms. Tucker announces that circle time will end after the class sings the ABC song, Jon begins to cry aloud. Mr. Lee reasons with Jon, but he repeatedly states that he wants to go home. Circle time ends. | Language expression/comprehension | |
| | Self-regulation | |
| | Safe/healthy behavior | |
| | Self-help skills | |
| | Gross motor skills | |
| | Fine motor skills | |
| | | |

**Comments:**
This is Jon's second week since returning to school after being out as a result of strep throat. His refusal to take part in group activities has been observed before, but not to the current level of resistance. Jon observed the other students interacting but refused to be an active participant. I sense that he feels more comfortable observing than actually participating today.

Jon usually responses to Ms. Tucker's one-on-one and/or personal request to join the group activities once asked, but during this observation, this technique was ineffective. This is not the norm for Jon.

Jon made several attempts to isolate and comfort himself. It seems that he seeks independence and control.

**Notes:**
The inability to console or redirect Jon's behavior had become more and more frequent over the last 2 weeks, even before he was out sick. I will continue to note times and frequency of upsets for Jon to determine

| What Actually Happened/What I Saw | Developmental Interpretation (Select 1 or 2 of the following) | |
|---|---|---|
| causes and triggers of disruptive behaviors. We will schedule a conference with his parents to determine whether they are witnessing some of the same responses from Jon. We will also discuss ways to support Jon even more. | | |

## ANECDOTAL RECORD

Child's name: _____     Date: _____

Observer: _____

| What Actually Happened/What I Saw | Developmental Interpretation (Select 1 or 2 of the following) | |
|---|---|---|
| | Interest in learning | |
| | Self-esteem/self-concept | |
| | Cultural acceptance | |
| | Problem solving | |
| | Interest in real-life mathematical concepts | |
| | Interactions with adults | |
| | Literacy | |
| | Interactions with peers | |
| | Language expression/comprehension | |
| | Self-regulation | |
| | Safe/healthy behavior | |
| | Self-help skills | |
| | Gross motor skills | |
| | Fine motor skills | |
| | | |
| | | |
| | | |
| | | |
| | | |
| | | |
| | | |
| | | |
| | | |
| | | |
| | | |
| | | |
| | | |
| | | |
| | | |
| | | |

## RUNNING RECORD

Another form of authentic assessment is the running record. It covers a longer time span and gives more information than an anecdotal record. Often it may have a specific developmental focus, such as "social interactions." A running record will give you information about other developmental areas because of its very detailed nature. This form of observation requires the caregiver to not be involved with children for several minutes while writing the observation. You will be setting yourself apart from the children and writing continuously, in as much detail as possible. You will write what the child does and says, by himself or herself and in interactions with other people and materials. Use objective phrases and avoid interpretative and judgmental language. Note that the format for this form of assessment has three columns. The left column is for writing the actual observations, and the right two columns are for connecting the observations to aspects of development. Remember to date all observations; this makes it possible to notice developmental change over time.

Child's name: **Sara**                                    Age: 7 yr. 5 mo.
Observer: Jorge                                             Date: July 27, 2006

## DEVELOPMENTAL FOCUS: SOCIAL INTERACTIONS WITH PEERS

| What Actually Happened/What I Saw | Developmental Interpretation (Select 1 or 2 of the following) | |
|---|---|---|
| Sara sits in the dramatic play area alone playing with the cash register. She pretends to pay for the groceries that she has in the shopping cart. Sara counts aloud, "one, two, three, five, eight dollars," while handing the money forward to the make-believe cashier. "I need some money back too," she says. Sara continues playing until she sees Ms. Jones reading to a group of students on the floor. Sara leaves her current activities and heads toward the group of children and Ms. Jones while saying, "I want to hear the story too! I want to hear the story too!" "Sure, you may join us, Sara," Ms. Jones replies. As Ms. Jones reads aloud, Sara interrupts, stating that she has a pet fish too, but it is orange, not yellow. Sara continues to interrupt, inserting comments like, "I like this part of the story." Ms. Jones asks Sara why she likes this part of the story? Sara replies, "I like him," pointing to the little turtle in the story. | Participates in cooperative activities | |
| | Early literacy/expressive language | X |
| | Expresses empathy | |
| | Communicates knowledge of growing skills | X |
| | Self-regulates/controls emotions | |
| | Stands up for own rights | X |
| | Asks for what he or she needs | |
| | Gross motor skills | X |
| | Math skill | |
| | Self-awareness | |
| | | |
| | | |
| | | |
| | | |
| | | |

| What Actually Happened/What I Saw | Developmental Interpretation (Select 1 or 2 of the following) | |
|---|---|---|
| Before Ms. Jones can comment, Sara tries to turn the page of the book, saying that she wants to see the last part of the story. Ms. Jones tells her that she and the other children are still reading this page. "We are almost there," says Ms. Jones. "Will you help me turn the page when I finish?" Sara refuses and skips off toward the art center, saying, "I want to go play now." Ms. Jones continues reading the story to the other children seated with her. Sara selects paper and two markers, one blue and the other yellow. She begins to draw with the yellow marker. Afterward, she colors the remaining space on the paper entirely blue. A male student comes over and asks, "What's that?" Sara replies, "You know. It's a fish swimming in the ocean." The other child looks at her and walks away. Sara writes her name on the drawing paper and then walks over to the art board and places it on the board. She moves toward the shelf and reaches to get more paper when she hears Ms. Jones call clean-up time. Sara puts the paper back on the shelf and says, "Lunchtime! Lunchtime! I'm hungry. I'm the line leader today." | | |

## CHECKLIST

A checklist is often used as a means of assessment because it is one of the easiest assessment tools to use. A checklist consists of a pre-determined list of clearly observable developmental criteria for which the observer indicates "yes" or "no." The observer reads the developmental criteria and makes a checkmark if the decision is a "yes." This form of assessment requires that no additional notes be recorded. Many teachers design their own checklists to fit the specific needs of their program. The following checklist is an example of one that might be used to assess social skills of children.

### SOCIAL SKILLS CHECKLIST

Child's name: _____         Age: (yr. mo.) _____
Observer's name: _____         Date: _____

| Skills | Dates |
|---|---|
| ☐ Desires to and can work near other children | |
| ☐ Interacts with other children | |
| ☐ Takes turns with other children | |
| ☐ Enters play with others in positive manner | |
| ☐ Shares materials and supplies | |
| ☐ Stands up for own rights in positive manner | |
| ☐ Forms friendships with peers | |
| ☐ Engages in positive commentary on other children's work | |
| ☐ Shows empathy | |
| ☐ Negotiates compromises with other children | |
| ☐ Demonstrates prosocial behavior | |
| ☐ Participates in cooperative group activities | |
| ☐ Resolves conflicts with adult prompts | |
| ☐ Resolves conflicts without adult prompts | |

Make checklists for each center in your classroom and hang them on clipboards. When you observe the children at play in each center, check off skills by placing a date in the appropriate box.

The last type of observation that a teacher should perform is a time or event sampling. These are similar in focus, but different too. A *time sampling* asks the teacher to set a timer and each time the timer goes off, the teacher looks at a particular child and writes down what the child is doing. Again, only the facts are written. The timer is set to go off every 10 minutes. The teacher will look at Johnny and see what he is doing when the timer sounds.

In this time sampling example, the teacher is observing Johnny to see how often he engages in literacy-related types of activities. The teacher is watching for his involvement in the following activities:

- language interchanges with other children

- the use of writing/drawing materials in learning centers

- interactions with books

- use of literacy games

- use of the listening center

The first time the timer goes off, the teacher observes that Johnny is sitting with another child in the book center. They are talking about the truck in the book and discussing which one is bigger. Therefore, in the chart that follows, the teacher will check off language interchanges with another child and interaction with books. The second time the timer sounds, the teacher observes that Johnny is making a sign for his building in the block area. He tells the other teacher that the sign says "stop" so that the other children will not tear his building down. He asks to color it red so that they will know it says "stop." For this occurrence, the teacher will check off the use of writing/drawing materials in learning centers. The teacher will continue to observe Johnny in 10-minute intervals to make accurate observations about how often he is involved in literacy-related activities.

**Example of Time Sampling Chart for Literacy-Related Involvement**

| Name of child: Johnny Doe | | | | | | |
| --- | :-: | :-: | :-: | :-: | :-: | :-: |
| **Literacy Activity** | **1** | **2** | **3** | **4** | **5** | **6** |
| Language interchange with another child or teacher | X | | | | | |
| Participation in writing/drawing activities | | X | | | | |
| Interactions with books | X | | | | | |
| Use of literacy games | | | | | | |
| Use of listening center | | | | | | |

As mentioned, an *event sampling* is similar, only the teacher looks at events instead of being directed by a timer. The teacher zeros in on an event and writes down all things that he or she sees pertaining to the event.

This event sampling is based on the observation of how a child might use the functions of language. The teacher is observing for the use of language for the following functions:

- verbalizes basic needs

- gives directions and persuades others

- talks about personal activities or interests

- asks questions

- solves problems verbally

- plans with others

- uses language to maintain relationships

- uses language imaginatively

## EVENT SAMPLE

| Antecedent | Behavior | Consequence |
| --- | --- | --- |
| Johnny is playing in the block area. Thomas walks over to begin playing with the blocks Johnny is using. | Johnny tells Thomas to stay away from the blocks he has already used to build his tower. He says, "See my sign. It says stop so that you cannot knock my building down." | Thomas slides over and uses other blocks to build close to the building that Johnny has built. Johnny has successfully used language to give directions and to solve problems. |
| Johnny gets up in somewhat of a hurry to leave group time. He has been fidgeting in his seat for a few minutes. | The teacher asks Johnny to sit down until the story is finished. Johnny tells the teacher that he really needs to go the bathroom and that he cannot wait. He says, "May I please go to the bathroom right now?" | Johnny goes to the bathroom and comes out to wash his hands, referring to the sign above the sink with a reminder of how to do so. Johnny has effectively used language to verbalize basic needs in an appropriate manner. |

Assessment and observation may seem overwhelming as you begin your career in early childhood. Do not shy away from it. Take the challenge and begin to look for the positive aspects of learning and mastering a new skill. Picture yourself as a student in your classroom and imagine what it is like to perfect something your teacher has just asked you to do. How does it make you feel? Now begin.

# CURRICULUM AND LESSON PLANS

- You have the day planned for outdoor activities and there is an unexpected rainstorm. What will you do?

- It is your day off and you get a call at the last minute to cover for a co-worker who is ill. You find out that nothing has been planned. What activities can you implement quickly?

- You were promised that the materials you needed for your planned art activity would be on site when you arrived at work, but there was a shipping delay and they are not there. What is an alternative activity you can easily set up and implement?

Being prepared at all times with a few back-up activities will make your job much less stressful. Some of the activities listed here require only a few materials that you might want to have on hand at all times.

## WHAT I LIKE TO DO AT SCHOOL?

**Developmental Focus:** Children will build prewriting skills by expressing their favorite thing to do at school in writing and drawing.

**Goal:** The children will be able to express their favorite thing to do at school with one to three written words and a drawing.

**Age Range:** three to six years old

**Materials:** drawing paper, drawing and writing materials and supplies

**Procedure:** Build motivation by discussing with the children what they like to do at school. Chart or write on the board the various responses to questions such as, "What is the one thing you like to do most at school?" and "Why do you like to do this activity or thing the most?"

Tell the children they are going to write and illustrate the thing they like most about school. Refer the group to the chart of responses to select an example (you can also use an example not listed on the chart). Model by drawing your favorite thing to do at school, such as reading a book or using blocks or counters to solve math problems. Then write at least two words to describe why you like to do this particular activity or event at school. Share your final drawing and written description with the class. Have the children complete the activity, providing guidance when needed. Be sure to have the children read to you and/or the class what they wrote about their picture and encourage the young authors to continue writing if they choose to do so. Conclude by reviewing the lesson objectives and by allowing the children to share with one another what they like to do most at school with the class.

## "I CAN" POEMS

**Developmental Focus:** Children will build language (speaking) skills by sharing their "I can" messages with others in the class.

**Goals:** Children will demonstrate their ability to state "I can" messages to their classmates.

**Age Range:** two to four years old

**Materials:** paper microphones (make out of rolled-up construction paper and cotton balls or use paper towel or tissue roll), a classroom or other learning environment that facilitates communication among the children

**Procedure:** Begin the lesson by using the paper microphones to build motivation; spark a conversation with statements such as, "At school, we all can do many wonderful things to learn from one another" or "Today, we are going to celebrate what we can do!" Model expectation by actually using the paper microphone to tell one of the children an "I can" message. Then, instruct that child to go tell another child an "I can" message. You may need to prompt the children by helping them to remember their messages.

Continue this activity until everyone has had a chance to complete the activity by sharing an "I can" message. Provide guidance when needed. Be sure to assist the children who experience trouble expressing their "I can" messages. Conclude by reviewing the lesson objectives and by having the children to make group "I can" messages.

**Extension:** Write out or have the children write out their "I can" messages and encourage them to illustrate them. Post the messages on an "I can" bulletin board.

## LET'S LISTEN

**Developmental Focus:** Children will build literary and listening skills by listening to a variety of songs and selecting their favorite to write about.

**Goals:** Children will listen to a variety of songs to select and write about their favorite songs to build literary and listening skills.

**Age Range:** five to eight years old

**Materials:** a variety of music selections, the equipment to play music selections, writing paper and materials

**Procedure:** Prepare the children by discussing what we all can learn from listening in general and from listening specifically to music. Chart or write on the board the various responses given during the discussion. Tell the children they are going to listen to and write about which song they like the most and why. Model expectation by writing an example of your favorite music selection and stating clearly why you selected this particular song. You may even want to play two songs for the group to vote on as a way to determine which song the children like the most. Encourage the children to provide their reasons for selecting this song; record their responses. Play different songs for the children. Depending on the age group, you may need to limit the number of song sections. (Gather appropriate music before the event.) Instruct the children to draw a happy face on a piece of paper if they like the music that was played. Have the children place their happy face beside the song they liked the most on the provided chart labeled, "Let's Listen!" Provide guidance when needed. Encourage the children to write why they like the selected song. Conclude by reviewing the lesson objectives and by sharing what the children wrote about their favorite song.

## READY TO READ RIGHT

**Developmental Focus:** Children will build prereading skills by recognizing letters and letter sounds.

**Goal:** The children will build prereading skills by recognizing letters and letter sounds of at least three letters.

**Age Range:** three to five years old

**Materials:** list of the alphabet, a copy of the "Alphabet Song," ABC matching card

**Procedure:** Review previous lessons and letters of the alphabet. Ask review questions to prepare the children for the next part of the lesson. Tell the children they are going to go on an alphabet hunt in the classroom and that they are going to find as many letters as they can by name in our class today. Tell them you want them to find at least three letters. Give the children time to wander around the classroom hunting for letters. Once a child has located and identified a letter by name and sound, check for accuracy. Encourage the children to locate, identify, and sound out three of the letters of the alphabet correctly. (Increase expectations for those who are ready.) Conclude by reviewing the lesson objectives and by allowing the children to point out were they located their letters.

## MATCH THE SOUND

**Developmental Focus:** auditory discrimination

**Goal:** The children will increase their skills in auditory discrimination by matching the sounds of the shakable plastic eggs.

**Age Range:** three to five years old

**Materials:** plastic eggs (same color) or other opaque hard plastic items that can be sealed; variety of items to be placed in plastic eggs, such as rice, beans, fish aquarium rocks, and so forth

**Procedure:** Place each of the items into a pair of eggs. Be sure to have the same amount of the item measured out so that the sound will be the same when the eggs are shaken. Seal the eggs and secure them with glue or tape. Mix the eggs up and have the children find the ones that sound the same by shaking the eggs. It is best if the children pick up two eggs at a time and then try to find the egg that matches one of the first pair. Continue this process until the children have matched all of the pairs of eggs. The reason that using the same color eggs is best is so that children do not become confused by color matching.

**Extension:** Use bells of different sizes and shapes. The children can sequence the bells by the loudest to the softest or by the pitch of the bells. The sequencing aspect of this activity takes auditory discrimination to the next level.

## WHAT IS THE ORDER?

**Developmental Focus:** sequencing skills

**Goal:** The children will improve their visual memory skills by sequencing the events of the story *Napping House.*

**Age Range:** three to six years old

**Materials:** the book *Napping House,* by Audrey Wood; flannel board; flannel board cutouts of the characters in the book

**Procedure:** After introducing and reading the story to the children, retell the story using the flannel board pieces. Have the children bring the flannel board pieces up to the board as they hear the corresponding part of the story. During center time, have the flannel board and the pieces along with the book in the library area. Encourage the children to go to the area with a friend and use the flannel board on their own to retell the story.

**Extension:** Leave out one of the flannel board pieces and recall the story with the children. See if they can figure out from memory which character is missing. This book can also be used for vocabulary development. Help the children think of words used to describe sleeping (for example, snoozing, dozing, slumbering).

## OBSTACLE COURSE WITH POSITIONAL WORDS

**Developmental Focus:** vocabulary development

**Goal:** The children will increase their understanding of positional words by following the directions as they proceed through the obstacle course. (Example: over, under, around, between, through, and so on.)

**Age Range:** three to five years old

**Materials:** items to make the obstacle course, such as sheets, chairs, crawl-through tubes or tunnels, hoops, balance beams, and masking tape

**Procedure:** Place the items strategically so that the children can follow the obstacle path. As you demonstrate how to use the obstacle course with the children, use the positional words to describe what they are to do. As the children go through the course on their own, move throughout the course and have them tell you what they are doing. To increase the interest for this activity, modify the look of the course to make it look like an ocean floor or a deep forest. Use your imagination and have fun with it!

**Extension:** This activity also has applications for children's development of spatial relationships (understanding their body in space). As they squeeze through the tube or as they find a partner to hop through the hoops with them, they gain a better understanding of how their body moves through space.

## PAIR IT UP

**Developmental Focus:** visual perception

**Goal:** The children will increase their visual perception skills by matching the items with the same wallpaper pattern.

**Age Range:** three to six years old

**Materials:** wallpaper samples cut out in any shape (shapes can be based on a theme; for example, sails for boats, mittens for winter)

**Procedure:** For a theme about oceans, consider having sails for boats cut out of various patterns of wallpaper. On each boat, glue a sample of the same wallpaper. Be sure the sample is large enough for the children to see the design on the wallpaper. Have the children match the sail to the boat with the same wallpaper design. For older children, the task is more challenging if the wallpaper designs are similar in color and patterns. For younger children or children who might have delays, it is best to use patterns that are different in color and design.

## PACKING MY LUNCH

**Developmental Focus:** purposeful listening

**Goal:** The children will improve their listening skills by packing the lunch box items according to the verbal directions of their partner.

**Age Range:** three to six years old

**Materials:** empty lunch box, pictures of items that would be packed for a picnic lunch

**Procedure:** Have each child identify each type of food or beverage pictured on the cutouts. Have one child name three items he or she would like to pack for a picnic. The second child may not pack the items until the list is complete. Once the list is complete, the second child will then pick up those items and put them into the lunch box. The first child can verify, from memory, that the items selected are correct. The children can take turns with this activity. The activity can be made more difficult by increasing the number of items selected.

**Extension:** To focus on visual memory, have the children study and try to memorize the items on the table. Then have one child close his or her eyes while the other one selects three items and puts them into the lunch box. Then the first child will open his or her eyes and try to guess what has been packed into the lunch box by deciding, based on memory, which of the items is now missing. This activity also has implications for nutrition education as you discuss or select healthy items for inclusion in the lunch box or picnic basket.

A number of Web sites offer sample lesson plans for teachers. When downloading lesson plans from the Internet or another source, be sure each plan includes:

- objective or goal of the lesson.
- materials needed.
- directions for the activity.
- appropriate age group.
- developmental appropriateness.

Check the Resources section of this manual for a list of Web sites with lesson plans and other free materials for teachers.

# MAKING CONNECTIONS THROUGH WEBBING

## SAMPLE FOR WEB DIAGRAM

Webbing activities are one way to integrate content areas so that they become more meaningful for children. According to brain-based learning principles, children learn better when new material is tied to prior learning and when content learned is connected in meaningful ways. Another advantage of webbing is that it can move teachers away from the inappropriate idea of using a new theme each week. The goal of learning is to dig deeply into topics instead of getting only a whirlwind overview. In designing a web, teachers can begin with a book or a topic that they and the children enjoy and find interesting. Choose activities that would facilitate learning in each of the content areas. Build literacy through the process. Be creative. The ideas presented here are just a sampling from which to get started. From the webbed activities, teachers can plan activities for several weeks.

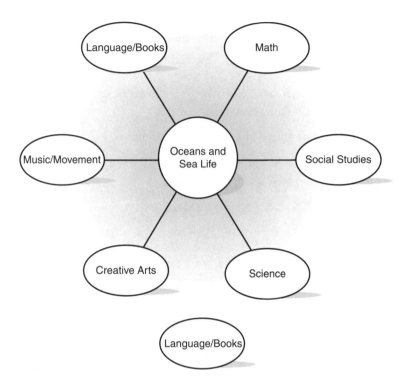

- Plan an obstacle course that represents an ocean. Use positional words throughout the course.

- After sharing the book *Swimmy,* have the children write or draw different endings to the story.

- Place books about sea life throughout all centers in the classroom.

- Use flannel boards and puppets to reenact and to retell stories about sea animals.

- Use magnets on the ends of short poles to have the children catch fish for objects that match in size, shape, or color. They can also draw a card and catch the fish that matches.

- Plan a matching game where the children use one-to-one correspondence to match sails to boats.

- Have children measure fish cutouts and sequence them by length.

- Plan an art activity where the children use fish stencils to add to their mural of the ocean.

- Have the children make sand paintings.

- Use creative dramatics to act out the story *Swimmy*.

- Plan a visit to a local aquarium or pet store.

- Do a sinking and floating activity and experiment with the effects of salt on sinking and floating objects.

- Make a wave tube.

- Have children move like different types of sea animals, for example, crabs, jellyfish, octopus, and so forth.

- Use songs about fishing, such as Hap Palmer's *Fishing Trip*.

- Listen to ocean sounds and have the children do creative movements with colorful scarves to signify the colors of coral in the ocean.

- Make a game where children match the types of animals to their habitats, for example, freshwater or salt water.

- Share a book with the children about how fish get from the ocean to the restaurant or to their table.

- Plan a fish market for the dramatic play area. At the same time, turn the block area into a fishing port.

# UNDERSTANDING THE DEVELOPMENT OF LANGUAGE AND LITERACY

Becoming effective communicators involves a process of developing skills in reading, writing, listening, and speaking. Because so much information gained today is obtained through the activity of viewing, several authors have added viewing to the list of skill areas important in the development of literacy. As we look at helping children become fluent communicators, it is important to examine primarily reading, writing, listening, and speaking. Reading and viewing will be considered together as the early reading behaviors of young children are related to the acquisition of information gained from viewing.

Planning a quality environment for the enhancement of literacy involves

- many opportunities for children to experience read-aloud stories, storytelling, and retellings.

- opportunities to sing, talk, and enjoy play with language.

- using writing and literacy throughout their play.

Literacy is *not* choosing a letter of the week. Literacy enhancement requires building an inviting and exciting environment and activities that build literacy into the fabric of everything that is done in the classroom in a meaningful way. It is much more exciting to learn about the letter *p* as a part of an exciting, in-depth investigation on popcorn than to have a new letter for the focus each week.

- It is the teacher's role to establish literacy as a source for enjoyment for the children.

- The teacher should model the pleasures of books, stories, and writing.

- The environment and activities should be carefully planned to enhance literacy skills through meaningful interactions with the many facets of language.

In the book *Literacy: The Creative Curriculum Approach* (2004), there are several suggested ways a teacher can ensure that literacy becomes a source of enjoyment for the children:

- Model literacy behaviors for the children, such as reading and talking about your favorite books and stories and favorite authors.

- Make story time pleasurable for the children.

- Capture children's interest before beginning to read aloud.

- Encourage children to enjoy books independently and allow them to request favorites at story time.

- Make books and reading strategies a part of the active participation during story time.

- Make the library area inviting so that children will want to interact with the books and materials there.

- Add books made by the children to the library area.

- During free choice time, go to the library area several times. Children often will migrate to where teachers are showing interest.

- Let children work together during literacy experiences. Children enjoy working in small groups or with partners.

- Work with families to make literacy experiences at home an interactive time of fun and enjoyment.

Many types of curriculum guides can be used effectively in planning quality programs for young children in the area of literacy. It is important to remember that a good curriculum looks at planning, arranging the environment, interacting with children, as well as using strategies to observe and document learning. A curriculum is not just a collection of lesson plans and activity plans. Those types of things are only one piece of a good curriculum. The *Creative Curriculum*, by Dianne Trister Dodge, is one example of a popular curriculum built around all of these important components. There is special attention given to literacy in the book titled *Literacy: The Creative Curriculum Approach* (2004). This book can be extremely helpful as teachers begin to understand how to build literacy skills into early childhood settings.

Any quality literacy program for young children must be built around the components of literacy. In *Literacy: The Creative Curriculum Approach* (2004), the components of reading, writing, listening, speaking, and viewing are incorporated into the following:

- literacy as a source of enjoyment

- vocabulary and language development

- phonological awareness (hearing and understanding the different sounds and language patterns that are spoken)

- knowledge of print

- letters and words

- comprehension

- understanding of books and other texts

## THE BEGINNINGS OF SYMBOLIC REPRESENTATION

Young children progress through different levels of understanding as they develop concepts of print and how symbols are used to represent thoughts. These stages can be seen as a snapshot of what children currently understand about written language.

The various stages of early writing reveal the desire of children to communicate. When adults honor children's attempts at writing, it leads to new discoveries and understandings as children experiment with letter forms and symbols as a way to describe their thoughts and feelings.

Like all developmental stages, the stages of early writing do not take place in a linear, clear-cut fashion. Children move in and out of stages in lulls and spurts. These transformations do not take place overnight. Rather, they occur over a long stretch of time and after many, many experiences with putting marks on paper in an informal and undirected manner. The early childhood teacher provides a variety of materials for use in writing and gives children many opportunities to practice writing throughout their day. When a child is in a print-rich environment where writing is modeled for the children and where the child is encouraged to experiment with writing in an informal and relaxed interactive setting, the child can progress naturally through the stages of symbolic representation.

It must *not* be concluded that "learning to write" or to make and recognize letters is a goal of the preschool program. *It is not!* Observations teachers make about children's progression through the stages of writing yield much information about children's understanding of the world and should be used for this purpose.

## BASIC ACTIVITIES TO PROMOTE LANGUAGE AND LITERACY SKILLS

### For Children 0–4 Years Old

Language Skills

- Use routines such as toileting, preparation for meals, or naps or transition times to talk to children; use nursery rhymes, finger plays, and conversations to extend language development.

- Provide pictures in places where children can see them and will talk about them with an adult or another child.

- Use a variety of labeling games with children, such as identifying body parts or labeling objects or events.

- Ensure that children have a variety of opportunities to experience new things. Ask questions about what they are seeing and observing. Encourage preschool children to draw pictures of what they have seen.

- Use good-quality literature so that children can connect with what is read and relate it to their world.

- Encourage children to take the lead in "reading" a familiar story to you by asking them questions; it is amazing how they will then begin to tell you the story.

- Encourage children to participate in dramatic play scenarios where they take the role of a book character or play out real-life scenarios, such as shopping for groceries.

- When rereading stories to children, point out interesting and new vocabulary. ("How many words can we think of to explain how the wind blows?") There are many good books to facilitate this.

Phonological Skills (Awareness of the Sounds in Language)

Use songs and word games with children that focus on rhyming or language sounds. Children have a natural interest in language, and the use of rhyming and nonsense words sparks their interests.

- Help children pick out words and sounds in their everyday world that begin or end alike. ("I'm thinking of a word that sounds like *paper* at the beginning, but this thing must be popped before I can eat it. What is my word?")

- Use books that use repeated sounds or rhyming words within the text. Children will enjoy supplying the missing words.

Speech Discrimination (Understanding the Differences in Similar-Sounding Words)

- Make a game of identifying pictures in books, especially for objects that sound similar, such as *goat* and *coat*. Also make picture cards and play a game of identifying the word you say. ("Find the picture of the coat. Now find the picture of the goat.")

- Have children play word games by changing the first sound in the word to make a new word. (Replace the "m" in *mat* with a "p" to make *pat*.) Matching these words with pictures also increases children's comprehension of vocabulary.

Auditory Discrimination (Training the Ear to Hear Slight Differences in Sounds)

- Plan activities that have children identify items by the sound they make. Use common items, such as bells, sandpaper, and so on.

- Have children identify the type of instrument played by matching it to the sound made by that instrument.

Understanding of Print (Beginning Awareness of the Use of Print, the Functions of Print, the Basic Concepts of Print and Grammar, Letter and Early Word Recognition)

- Provide print-rich environments:
  - age-appropriate, high-quality children's literature

- alphabet manipulative toys: alphabet blocks and magnetic letters

- use of functional print (print with a purpose children can understand) in the environment as a part of the regular routine

- readily accessible writing tools

- literacy in every center in the classroom (Remember: Literacy involves reading, writing, listening, speaking, and viewing.)

■ Take advantages of opportunities to point out the use of print in the child's world.

■ Use common logos with which the children are familiar, such as fast food or cereal labels.

■ Model writing throughout the day in a useful and purposeful way for the children.

■ Give children an opportunity to imitate writing.

■ Help children see and understand different types of print and their purposes (for example, grocery lists, cards, menus).

■ Have children use print to answer questions in their world (for example, have them use the weather report from the newspaper to decide what to wear outside).

■ After repeated readings of books, take opportunities to point out how punctuation is used in the book. (The first time children experience a story, it should be for the joy of the story.)

■ Do many games and transition activities that use the initial letters of the children's names to make the use of letters meaningful. (For example, as children leave circle time, sing a song such as "If your name begins with _____, you may go." Be sure to point to the letter or hold the letter up as you sing.)

Book Awareness and Sense of Story*

- When reading high-quality, age-appropriate books to young children, remember the value of repeated readings for depth of appreciation and understanding.

- Provide opportunities to use puppets and flannel boards to retell or act out stories.

- Use audio recordings of books as a way for children to hear and "picture read" favorite stories independently.

- Encourage children to use drawing to experience their favorite stories and characters.

- Create a warm and inviting environment for sharing stories.

- Create an inviting book center that changes with the focus of the classroom and the interest of the children. Do not let the book center be a stagnant place where children do not wish to go. Try filling a small plastic swimming pool with pillows so that children can cuddle up with a favorite book.

- Use good literature as a regular part of planning activities for the children.

---

*Some material from this section was adapted from Burns, S. M., Griffin, P., & Snow, C. E. (Eds.). (1999). *Starting out right: A guide to promoting children's reading success.* Washington, DC: National Academy Press.

# BOOKS FOR CHILDREN

Reading aloud is a wonderful gift you can give to children. Through sharing an interesting book, you introduce them to a world they might not otherwise be able to visit. You can travel anywhere you like; you can have experiences that are outside the realm of your current environment; you can participate in wonderful fantasies; you can be saddened, then uplifted.

Children's desire to read and the ability to do so is fostered by being read to as soon as they are born. Even babies can enjoy looking at picture books and hearing simple stories. Preschoolers love to have favorite books read to them repeatedly. As children move into the school years, they can sustain their interest in longer books that are divided into chapters. When they realize the joy that comes from good books, they are more motivated to read on their own.

Many textbooks provide suggestions for setting up reading corners and providing books for children to read by themselves. This section will focus on books that you can read aloud to children in small or large groups. Remember that the more you read, the better you will become at doing so. When the books have been enjoyed in a group setting, add them to the book corner for children to read alone. In addition, teachers often create lending arrangements where children can take books home for their parents to read and then return. Teachers who believe in the importance of reading choose the best of children's literature and involve families in reading.

## HOW TO GET CHILDREN TO LISTEN AND WANT MORE

- Schedule time each day for reading, maybe toward the end of the day, when children are tired and will enjoy the inactivity; make sure the setting is comfortable.

- Choose books that you also enjoy, perhaps one you read as a child; preview the book before presenting it to the children in case there are passages you want to shorten.

- The first time you read a book, state the title and author. Research for interesting facts about the author to share with the children. If there is an illustrator, include that information as well.

- If you are reading to a large group, position yourself so that you are slightly higher than the children so that your voice will project more easily.

- If you are reading to a small group, sit among them in a more intimate placement, which will draw them to you and the book.

- Occasionally stop and ask, "What do you think is going to happen next?"

- Read at a pace that allows children to build mental images of the characters or setting; change your pace to match the action of the story. Slow your pace and lower you voice during a suspenseful spot and then speed up when the action does.

- Allow time for discussion only if children wish to do so. Let them voice fears, ask questions, or share their thoughts about the book. Do not turn it into a quiz or need to interpret the story.

- Practice reading aloud, trying to vary your expression or tone of voice.

- Create a display of images or information pertaining to the book you are reading. A map will allow children to pinpoint places mentioned in the story. Pictures, charts, or timelines will also add to the display. Objects or foods mentioned in the book add another dimension.

- Find a stopping place each day that will create suspense so that the children are eager to get back to the book the next day.

- When you pick up the book the next day, ask the children if they remember what had happened just before you stopped reading.

## WHAT NOT TO DO

- Do not read a book you do not enjoy; your feelings will be sensed by the children.

- Do not read a book when it becomes obvious that it was a poor choice; previewing the book before presenting it to the children can minimize these kinds of mistakes.

- Do not choose a book with which some of the children are already familiar; they may have heard it at home or seen a version on television or at the movies.

- Do not start a book unless you have enough time to read more than a few pages.

- Do not be fooled by awards. Just because a book has received a national book award does not mean that it is suitable for your particular group of children.

- Do not impose on the children your own interpretations or reactions to the story. Let them express their own understanding and feelings.

## 100 GREAT PICTURE BOOKS*

*Abulea,* by Arthur Dorros. Illustrated by Elisa Kleven. Dutton

*Alexander and the Terrible, Horrible, No Good, Very Bad Day,* by Judith Virost. Illustrated by Ray Cruz. Atheneum.

*Animals Should Definitely Not Wear Clothing,* by Ron Barrett. Atheneum.

*Anansi and the Moss-Covered Rock,* by Eric A. Kimmel. Illustrated by Janet Steven. Holiday House.

*Andy and the Lion,* by Janet Stevens. Holiday House.

---

*Compiled by the New York Public Library.

*Ben's Trumpet,* by Rachel Isadora. Greenwillow.

*Blueberries for Sal,* by Robert McCloskey. Viking.

*The Bossy Gallito: A Traditional Cuban Folk Tale,* retold by Lucia M. Gonzalez. Illustrated by Lulu Delacre. Scholastic.

*Bread and Jam for Frances,* by Russell Hoban. Illustrated by Lillian Hoban. HarperCollins.

*Caps for Sale: A Tale of a Peddler, Some Monkeys and Their Monkey Business,* by Esphyr Slobodkina. HarperCollins.

*The Carrot Seed,* by Ruth Krauss. Illustrated by Crockett Johnson. HarperCollins.

*A Chair for My Mother,* by Vera B. Williams. Greenwillow.

*Chicka Chicka Boom Boom,* by Bill Martin, Jr., and John Archambault. Illustrated by Lois Ehlert. Simon and Schuster.

*Corduroy,* by Don Freeman. Viking.

*Curious George,* by H. A. Rey. Houghton.

*The Day Jimmy's Boa Ate the Wash,* by Trinka H. Noble. Illustrated by Steven Kellogg. Dial.

*Dear Zoo,* by Rod Campbell. Simon & Schuster.

*Cotor De Soto,* by William Steig. Farrar.

*Farmer Duck,* by Martin Waddell. Illustrated by Helen Oxenbery. Candlewick Press.

*The Fortune-Tellers,* by Lloyd Alexander. Illustrated by Trina Schart Hyman. Dutton.

*Freight Train,* by Donald Crews. Greenwillow.

*George and Martha,* by James Marshall. Houghton.

*Go Away, Big Green Monster,* by Ed Emberley. Little, Brown.

*Good Night, Gorilla,* by Peggy Tathmann. Putnam.

*Goodnight Moon,* by Margaret W. Brown. Illustrated by Clement Hurd. HarperCollins.

*Grandfather's Journey,* by Allen Say. Houghton.

*Happy Birthday, Moon,* by Frank Asch. Simon & Schuster.

*Harold and the Purple Crayon,* by Crockett Johnson. HarperCollins.

*Harry and the Dirty Dog,* by Gene Zion. Illustrated by Margaret Graham, HarperCollins.

*Henny Penny,* illustrated by Paul Galdone. Clarion.

*Horton Hatches the Egg,* by Dr. Seuss. Random House.

*I Know an Old Lady Who Swallowed a Fly,* illustrated by Glen Rounds. Holiday House.

*If You Give a Mouse a Cookie,* by Laura J. Numeroff. Illustrated by Felicia Bond. HarperCollins

*Is It Red? Is It Yellow? Is It Blue? An Adventure in Color,* by Tana Hoban. Greenwillow.

*It Could Always Be Worse: A Yiddish Folktale,* retold and illustrated by Margot Zemach. Farrar.

*John Henry,* by Julius Lester. Illustrated by Jerry Pinkney. Dial.

*The Judge: An Untrue Tale,* by Harve Zemach. Illustrated by Margot Zemack. Viking.

*Julius,* by Angela Johnson. Illustrated by Dav Pilkey. Orchard.

*Komodo!* By Peter Sis. Greenwillow.

*Leo the Late Bloomer,* by Robert Draus. Illustrated by Jose Aruego. HarperCollins.

*Little Blue and Little Yellow,* by Leo Lionni. Astor-Honor.

*The Little Dog Laughed and Other Nursery Rhymes,* by Lucy Cousins. Dutton.

*The Little Old Lady Who Was Not Afraid of Anything,* by Linda Williams. Illustrated by Megan Lloyd. HarperCollins.

*Little Red Riding Hood,* retold and illustrated by Paul Galdone. McGraw-Hill.

*Lunch,* by Denise Fleming. Holt.

*Lyle, Lyle, Crocodile,* by Bernard Waber. Houghton.

*Madeline,* by Ludwig Bemelmans. Viking.

*Maisie Goes Swimming,* by Lucy Cousins. Little, Brown.

*Make Way for Ducklings,* by Robert McCloskey. Viking.

*Martha Calling,* by Susan Meddaugh. Houghton.

*Mike Mulligan and His Steam Shovel,* by Virginia L. Burton. Houghton.

*Millions of Cats,* by Wanda Gag. Putman.

*Miss Nelson Is Missing,* by Harry Allrad and James Marshall. Illustrated by James Marshall. Houghton.

*Mr. Grumpy's Outing,* by John Burningham. Holt.

*The Monkey and the Crocodile,* retold and illustrated by Paul Galdone. Clarion.

*Morris' Disappearing Bag,* by Rosemary Wells. Dial.

*Mouse Paint,* by Ellen S. Walsh. Harcourt.

*Mufaro's Beautiful Daughters: An African Tale,* retold and illustrated by John Steptoe. Lothrop.

*Mushroom in the Rain,* adapted from the Russian tale of V. Suteyev by Mirra Ginsburg. Illustrated by Jose Aruego and Ariane Dewey. Simon & Schuster.

*The Napping House,* by Audrey Wood. Illustrated by Don Wood. Harcourt.

*Officer Buckle and Gloria,* by Peggy Rathmann. Putman.

*Old Black Fly,* by Jim Aylesworth. Illustrated by Stephen Gammell. Holt.

*Over in the Meadow,* by John Langstaff. Illustrated by Feodor Rojankovsky. Harcourt.

*Owen,* by Kevin Henkes. Greenwillow.

*Papa, Please Get the Moon for Me,* by Eric Carle. Simon & Schuster.

*Perez and Martina,* by Pura Belpre. Illustrated by Carlos Sanchez. Viking.

*Pierre: A Cautionary Tale,* by Maurice Sendak. HarperCollins.

*The Polar Express,* by Chris Van Allsburg. Houghton.

*The Random House Book of Mother Goose: A Treasury of 386 Timeless Nursery Rhymes,* selected and illustrated by Arnold Lobel. Random House.

*Rosie's Walk,* by Pat Hutchins. Simon & Schuster.

*Round Trip,* by Ann Jonas. Greenwillow.

*Rumpelstiltskin,* retold and illustrated by Paul O. Zelinsky. Dutton.

*Seven Blind Mice,* by Ed Young. Putman.

*The Snowy Day,* by Ezra Jack Keats. Viking.

*Stone Soup,* retold and illustrated by Marcia Brown. Simon & Schuster.

*The Story of Babar, the Little Elephant,* by Jean De Brunhoff. Random House.

*The Story of Ferdinand,* by Munro Leaf. Illustrated by Robert Lawson. Viking.

*Strega Nona,* by Tomi De Paola. Simon & Schuster.

*Swamp Angel,* by Ann Isaacs. Illustrated by Paul O. Zelinsky. Dutton.

*Swimmy,* by Leo Lionni. Knopf.

*Sylvester and the Magic Pebble,* by William Steig. Simon & Schuster.

*The Tale of Peter Rabbit,* by Beatrix Potter, Warne.

*Ten, Nine, Eight,* by Molly Bang. Greenwillow.

*There's a Nightmare in My Closet,* by Mercer Mayer. Dial.

*The Three Billy Goats Gruff,* by P. C. Asbjfrnsen and J. E. Moe. Illustrated by Marcia Brown. Harcourt.

*The Three Robbers,* by Tomi Ungerer. Atheneum.

*Tikki Tikki Tembo,* retold by Arlene Mosel, Illustrated by Blair Lent. Holt.

*The True Story of the Three Little Pigs,* by A. Wolf as told to John Sciesza. Illustrated by Lane Smith. Viking.

*Tuesday,* by David Wiesner. Houghton.

*Two of Everything: A Chinese Folktale,* retold and illustrated by Lily Toy Hong. Whitman.

*The Very Hungry Caterpillar,* by Eric Carle. Philomel.

*We're Going on a Bear Hunt,* retold by Michael Rosen. Illustrated by Helen Oxenbury. McElderry.

*The Wheels on the Bus,* adapted and illustrated by Paul O. Zelinsky. Dutton.

*When I Was Young in the Mountains,* by Cynthia Rylant. Illustrated by Diane Goode. Dutton.

*Where the Wild Things Are,* by Maurice Sendak. HarperCollins.

*Where's Spot?* by Eric Hill. Putnam.

*Whistle for Willie,* by Ezra Jack Keats. Viking.

*Why Mosquitoes Buzz in People's Ears: A West African Tale,* retold by Verna Aardema. Illustrated by Leo and Dianne Dillon. Dial.

*Zomo the Rabbit: A Trickster Tale from West Africa,* retold and illustrated by Gerald McDermott. Harcourt.

## CALDECOTT MEDAL AWARD WINNERS:

The Caldecott Award is an award given each year to a picture book with outstanding illustrations.

2005: *Kitten's First Full Moon,* by Kevin Henkes (Greenwillow Books/HarperCollins)

2004: *The Man Who Walked between the Towers,* by Mordicai Gerstein (Roaring Brook Press/Millbrook Press)

2003: *My Friend Rabbit,* by Eric Rohmann (Roaring Brook Press/Millbrook Press)

2002: *The Three Pigs,* by David Wiesner (Clarion/Houghton Mifflin)

2001: *So You Want to Be President?* Illustrated by David Small; text by Judith St. George (Philomel Books)

2000: *Joseph Had a Little Overcoat,* Simms Taback (Viking)

1999: *Snowflake Bentley,* Illustrated by Mary Azarian; text by Jacqueline Briggs Martin (Houghton)

1998: *Rapunzel,* by Paul O. Zelinsky (Dutton)

1997: *Golem,* by David Wisniewski (Clarion)

1996: *Officer Buckle and Gloria,* by Peggy Rathmann (Putnam)

1995: *Smoky Night,* illustrated by David Diaz; text by Eve Bunting (Harcourt)

1994: *Grandfather's Journey,* by Allen Say; text edited by Walter Lorraine (Houghton)

1993: *Mirette on the High Wire,* by Emily Arnold McCully (Putnam)

1992: *Tuesday,* by David Wiesner (Clarion Books)

1991: *Black and White,* by David Macaulay (Houghton)

1990: *Lon Po Po: A Red-Riding Hood Story from China,* by Ed Young (Philomel)

1989: *Song and Dance Man,* illustrated by Stephen Gammell; text by Karen Ackerman (Knopf)

1988: *Owl Moon,* illustrated by John Schoenherr; text by Jane Yolen (Philomel)

1987: *Hey, Al,* illustrated by Richard Egielski; text by Arthur Yorinks (Farrar)

1986: *The Polar Express,* by Chris Van Allsburg (Houghton)

1985: *Saint George and the Dragon,* illustrated by Trina Schart Hyman; text retold by Margaret Hodges (Little, Brown)

1984: *The Glorious Flight: Across the Channel with Louis Bleriot,* by Alice and Martin Provensen (Viking)

1983: *Shadow,* translated and illustrated by Marcia Brown; original text in French by Blaise Cendrars (Scribner)

1982: *Jumanji,* by Chris Van Allsburg (Houghton)

1981: *Fables,* by Arnold Lobel (Harper)

1980: *Ox-Cart Man,* illustrated by Barbara Cooney; text by Donald Hall (Viking)

1979: *The Girl Who Loved Wild Horses,* by Paul Goble (Bradbury)

1978: *Noah's Ark,* by Peter Spier (Doubleday)

1977: *Ashanti to Zulu: African Traditions,* illustrated by Leo and Diane Dillon; text by Margaret Musgrove (Dial)

1976: *Why Mosquitoes Buzz in People's Ears,* illustrated by Leo and Diane Dillon; text retold by Verna Aardema (Dial)

1975: *Arrow to the Sun,* by Gerald McDermott (Viking)

1974: *Duffy and the Devil,* illustrated by Margot Zemach; text retold by Harve Zemach (Farrar)

1973: *The Funny Little Woman,* illustrated by Blair Lent; text retold by Arlene Mosel (Dutton)

1972: *One Fine Day*, retold and illustrated by Nonny Hogrogian (Macmillan)

1971: *A Story A Story*, retold and illustrated by Gail E. Haley (Atheneum)

1970: *Sylvester and the Magic Pebble*, by William Steig (Windmill Books)

1969: *The Fool of the World and the Flying Ship*, illustrated by Uri Shulevitz; text retold by Arthur Ransome (Farrar)

1968: *Drummer Hoff*, illustrated by Ed Emberley; text adapted by Barbara Emberley (Prentice Hall)

1967: *Sam, Bangs & Moonshine*, by Evaline Ness (Holt)

1966: *Always Room for One More*, illustrated by Nonny Hogrogian; text by Sorche Nic Leodhas, pseud. [Leclair Alger] (Holt)

1965: *May I Bring a Friend?* illustrated by Beni Montresor; text by Beatrice Schenk de Regniers (Atheneum)

1964: *Where the Wild Things Are*, by Maurice Sendak (Harper)

1963: *The Snowy Day*, by Ezra Jack Keats (Viking)

1962: *Once a Mouse*, retold and illustrated by Marcia Brown (Scribner)

1961: *Baboushka and the Three Kings*, illustrated by Nicolas Sidjakov; text by Ruth Robbins (Parnassus)

1960: *Nine Days to Christmas*, illustrated by Marie Hall Ets; text by Marie Hall Ets and Aurora Labastida (Viking)

1959: *Chanticleer and the Fox*, illustrated by Barbara Cooney; text adapted from Chaucer's *Canterbury Tales* by Barbara Cooney (Crowell)

1958: *Time of Wonder*, by Robert McCloskey (Viking)

1957: *A Tree Is Nice*, illustrated by Marc Simont; text by Janice Udry (Harper)

1956: *Frog Went A-Courtin'*, illustrated by Feodor Rojankovsky; text retold by John Langstaff (Harcourt)

1955: *Cinderella, or the Little Glass Slipper*, illustrated by Marcia Brown; text translated from Charles Perrault by Marcia Brown (Scribner)

1954: *Madeline's Rescue,* by Ludwig Bemelmans (Viking)

1953: *The Biggest Bear,* by Lynd Ward (Houghton)

1952: *Finders Keepers,* illustrated by Nicolas, pseud. [Nicholas Mordvinoff]; text by Will, pseud. [William Lipkind] (Harcourt)

1951: *The Egg Tree,* by Katherine Milhous (Scribner)

1950: *Song of the Swallows,* by Leo Politi (Scribner)

1949: *The Big Snow,* by Berta and Elmer Hader (Macmillan)

1948: *White Snow, Bright Snow,* illustrated by Roger Duvoisin; text by Alvin Tresselt (Lothrop)

1947: *The Little Island,* illustrated by Leonard Weisgard; text by Golden MacDonald, pseud. [Margaret Wise Brown] (Doubleday)

1946: *The Rooster Crows,* by Maude and Miska Petersham (Macmillan)

1945: *Prayer for a Child,* illustrated by Elizabeth Orton Jones; text by Rachel Field (Macmillan)

1944: *Many Moons,* illustrated by Louis Slobodkin; text by James Thurber (Harcourt)

1943: *The Little House,* by Virginia Lee Burton (Houghton)

1942: *Make Way for Ducklings,* by Robert McCloskey (Viking)

1941: *They Were Strong and Good,* by Robert Lawson (Viking)

1940: *Abraham Lincoln,* by Ingri and Edgar Parin d'Aulaire (Doubleday)

1939: *Mei Li,* by Thomas Handforth (Doubleday)

1938: *Animals of the Bible, A Picture Book,* illustrated by Dorothy P. Lathrop; text selected by Helen Dean Fish (Lippincott)

## PRESCHOOL PICKS

A listing of preschool book selections is available. The books are categorized by topics, such as families, feelings, art, music, and many more.

Complied by Partnerships for Inclusion of the Frank Porter Graham Center of the University of North Carolina–Chapel Hill, North Carolina (http://www.fpg.unc.edu). Select *More Requested Pages, Partnerships for Inclusion, Products, Preschool Picks.*

*Dr. Seuss Board Books,* by Dr. Seuss. Everyone's favorite titles, from *Dr. Seuss's ABC* to *Green Eggs and Ham.* Babies will love to hear the lyrical rhythm of the words.

*Goodnight Moon,* by Margaret Wise Brown. A beloved bedtime classic.

*Wee Pudgy Board Books,* by Putnam Publishing. Good photo board books for the little hands.

*Snapshot Series* and *Touch and Feel* Series Board Books, by Dorling Kindersley (DK) Publishing. Has bright colors and exciting textures.

*Baby Faces* Series, by Scholastic. Diverse photos of babies doing familiar games.

*Red Blue Yellow Shoe,* by Tana Hoban. Brightly colored objects that are easily recognized by babies.

*Baby Animals* and *Zoom Zoom,* by K. Warube. Exciting pictures of animals and objects.

*Flower in the Garden* and other titles, by Lucy Cousins. Cloth and vinyl books that can be washed. Include easily recognized objects.

*Spot* Series, by Putnum Publishing. Soft-touch books that can be used in the bath or any time.

*Hippety-Hop Hippety Hey: Growing Rhymes from Birth to Age Three,* by Opal Dunn and Sally Anne Lambert. Collection of rhymes with directions for use and categories according to age.

*Anansi and the Moss Covered Rock,* by Eric Kimmel. This story is one of many by Eric Kimmel that build around the trickery of Anansi the spider. This tale is based on African folklore.

*Elizabeti's Doll,* by Stephanie Stuve-Bodeen. In this book, when Elizabeti's mother has a new baby, Elizabeti does not have a doll to care for. She cares for a rock whose name is Eva, just as her mother cares for the baby. Young children can relate to the book as Eva disappears.

*Friends Together, More Alike Than Different,* by Rochelle Burnett. This book is 17″ by 11″ and has lovely photos of children with and without special needs having fun together. The pages can be used as posters. The book provides some suggestions for teachers to help children better understand special needs.

*Grandfather Counts,* by Andrea Cheng. Helen has mixed emotions when her grandfather arrives from China. She will have to give up her bedroom. Despite all of the changes, Helen and her grandfather develop a relationship that rises above language barriers.

*How Are You Peeling?* by Saxton Freymann and Joost Elffers. This beautifully illustrated book used photographs of fruits and vegetables to help children understand moods. This book is a good way to bridge emotional health to nutrition and to artwork.

*Ira Sleeps Over,* by Bernard Waber. This book tells the story of a young boy who is uncomfortable taking his special item that he sleeps with to his friend's house. His sibling picks on him, but he takes it anyway, only to discover that his friend also has a special item to which he is attached.

*Rolling Along with Goldilocks and the Three Bears,* by Cindy Meyers. This book is a version of the baby bear who must use a wheelchair to get around. The book helps children see similarities and differences among all children.

*The Kissing Hand,* by Audrey Penn. This is a touching book in which Chester's mother plants a kiss in the middle of his palm so that when he feels sad or lonely, she can always be with him. This book is really good for helping children get through transition times.

*The Rainbow Fish,* by Marcus Pfister. This book uses a fish with shinny scales to help children understand the importance of sharing. The story has a good moral, and the glittering fins easily catch the attention of the children.

*Three Star Billy,* by Pat Hutchins. This book is a fun story about a little monster who does not want to go to school. He soon learns that at school, he can do all of the things that he enjoys doing. The children will love the animation of Billy, the monster. This is a good book to use at the beginning of the school year as children are transitioning into preschool.

# DEVELOPMENTALLY APPROPRIATE PRACTICE

The National Association for the Education of Young Children's (NAEYC's) first position statement on developmentally appropriate practice had two main motivations:

- The process of accrediting centers required widely accepted and specific definitions of what constituted excellent practices in early childhood education.

- There was a proliferation of programs that had inappropriate practices and expectations for their children, largely based on premature academic learning.

The original position statement did enhance the early childhood profession, although it was not received with universal acceptance, so a revised position statement clarified some of the previous misunderstandings and expanded the vision of good practices.

It is important to keep the principles firmly in mind when making professional decisions. It is also important to use the statement in conversations with others regarding appropriate practices. Colleagues, administrators, and family members all have their individual understandings of what to do with young children. It is therefore useful for every teacher to have a copy of the position statement. In a conversation, you can use the position statement to replace the idea of personal opinions with the weight of the professional body of knowledge. The complete statement, *Developmentally Appropriate Practice in Early Childhood Programs,* Revised Edition (NAEYC, 1997), can be found at http://www.naeyc.org; click on *Information About NAEYC,* then select *Position Statements* and then *Developmentally Appropriate Practice.* The introduction follows.

## DEVELOPMENTALLY APPROPRIATE PRACTICE IN EARLY CHILDHOOD PROGRAMS SERVING CHILDREN FROM BIRTH THROUGH AGE 8

### A Position Statement for the National Association for the Education of Young Children, Adopted July 1996

This statement defines and describes principles of developmentally appropriate practice in early childhood programs for administrators, teachers, parents, policy makers, and others who make decisions about the care and education of young children. An early childhood program is any group program in a center, school, or other facility that serves children from birth through age eight. Early childhood programs include child care centers, family child care homes, private and public preschools, kindergartens, and primary-grade schools.

The early childhood profession is responsible for establishing and promoting standards of high-quality, professional practice in early childhood programs. These standards must reflect current knowledge and shared beliefs about what constitutes high-quality, developmentally appropriate early childhood education in the context within which services are delivered.

## GUIDELINES FOR DEVELOPMENTALLY APPROPRIATE PRACTICE

NAEYC's developmentally appropriate practice guidelines can be implemented in your daily work with children:

■ Create a caring environment among children and adults.
*Children*
- learn personal responsibility.
- develop constructive relationships with others.
- respect individual and cultural differences.

*Adults*
- get to know each child, taking into account individual differences and developmental level.
- adjust the pace and content of the curriculum so that children can be successful most of the time.
- bring each child's culture and language into the setting.
- expect children to be tolerant of others' differences.

■ The curriculum and schedule allow children to select and initiate their own activities.
*Children*
- learn through active involvement in a variety of learning experiences.
- build independence by taking on increasing responsibilities.
- initiate their own activities to follow their interests.

*Adults*
- provide a variety of materials and activities that are concrete and real.
- provide a variety of workplaces and work spaces.

- arrange the environment so that children can work alone or in groups.
- extend children's learning by posing problems and asking thought-provoking questions.
- add complexity to tasks as needed.
- model, demonstrate, and provide information so that children can progress in their learning.

■ The program is organized and integrated so that children develop a deeper understanding of key concepts and skills. *Children*
- engage in activities that reflect their current interests.
- plan and predict outcomes of their research.
- share information and knowledge with others.

*Adults*
- plan related activities and experiences that broaden children's knowledge and skills.
- design curriculum to foster important skills such as literacy and numeracy.
- adapt instruction for children who are ahead or behind age-appropriate expectations.
- plan curriculum so that children achieve important developmental goals.

■ Activities and experiences *help* children develop a positive self-image within a democratic community. *Children*
- learn through reading books about other cultures.
- read about current events and discuss how these relate to different cultures.
- accept differences among their peers, including children with disabilities.

*Adults*
- provide culturally diverse and nonsexist activities and materials that foster children's self-identity.
- design the learning environment so that children can learn new skills while using their native language.
- allow children to demonstrate their learning using their own language.

■ Activities and experiences develop children's awareness of the importance of community involvement. *Children*
- are ready and eager to learn about the world outside their immediate environment.

- are open to considering different ways of thinking or doing things.
- can benefit from contact with others outside their homes or child care setting.

*Adults*
- encourage awareness of the community at large.
- plan experiences in facilities within the community.
- bring outside resources and volunteers into the child care setting.
- encourage children to plan their involvement based on their own interests.

# PROFESSIONAL ORGANIZATIONS

When looking to further your development, a professional organization is a great place to start. There are several organizations available, some of which even have state or local affiliates.

**National Association for the Education of Young Children (NAEYC)**
1509 16th Street, NW
Washington, DC 20036
800-424-2460
http://www.naeyc.org
E-mail: membership@naeyc.org

*Specific membership benefits:*
Comprehensive members receive all the benefits of regular membership described here plus will annually receive five or six books immediately after their release by NAEYC.

*Regular and student members receive*

- six issues of *Young Children,* which includes timely articles on pertinent issues, as well as suggestions and strategies for enhancing children's learning.

- reduced registration fees at NAEYC-sponsored local and national conferences and seminars.

- discounted prices on hundreds of books, videos, brochures, and posters from NAEYC's extensive catalog of materials.

- access to the *Members Only* Web site, including links to additional resources and chat sites for communication with other professionals.

### National Association of Child Care Professionals (NACCP)
P.O. Box 90723
Austin, TX 78709
800-537-1118
http://www.naccp.org

*Specific membership benefits:*

**Management Tools of the Trade™.** Your membership provides complete and FREE access (a $79 value) to these effective management tools that provide technical assistance in human resource management. In addition, members will receive NACCP's quarterly trade journals, Professional Connections, Teamwork, and Caring for Your Children, *to help you stay* on top of hot issues in child care. Each edition also includes a Tool of the Trade™.

### National Child Care Association (NCCA)
1016 Rosser St.
Conyers, GA 30012
800-543-7161
http://www.nccanet.org

*Specific membership benefits:*

■ As the only recognized voice in Washington, DC, NCCA has great influence on our legislators.

■ Professional development opportunities are available.

### Association for Education International (ACEI)
The Olney Professional Building
17904 Georgia Avenue, Suite 215
Olney, MD 20832
Phone: 800-423-2563 or 301-570-2122
Fax: 301-570-2212
http://www.acei.org

ACEI is an international organization dedicated to promoting the best educational practices throughout the world.

*Specific membership benefits:*

■ workshops and travel/study tours abroad

■ four issues per year of the journals *Childhood Education* and *Journal of Research in Childhood Education*

- hundreds of resources for parents and teachers, including books, pamphlets, audio tapes, and videotapes

**National AfterSchool Association (NAA)**
1137 Washington Street
Boston, MA 02124
Phone: 617-298-5012
Fax: 617-298-5022
http://www.naaweb.org

NAA is a national organization dedicated to providing information, technical assistance, and resources concerning children in out-of-school programs. Members include teachers, policy makers, and administrators representing all public, private, and community-based sectors of after-school programs.

*Specific member benefits:*

- a subscription to the NAA journal *School-Age Review*

- a companion membership in state affiliates

- discounts on NAA publications and products

- discount on NAA annual conference registration

- opportunity to be an NAA accreditation endorser

- access to public policy representatives in Washington, DC

## OTHER ORGANIZATIONS TO CONTACT

Children's Defense Fund
25 E. St. NW
Washington, DC 20001
202-628-8787
http://www.childrensdefense.org

Council for Exceptional Children
1110 N. Glebe Road, Suite 300
Arlington, VA 22201
888-CEC-SPED
http://www.cec.sped.org
Journal: *CEC Today*

International Reading Association
800 Barksdale Road
P.O. Box 8139
Newark, DE 19714
800-336-READ
http://www.reading.org
Journal: *The Reading Teacher*

International Society for the Prevention of Child Abuse and Neglect
25 W. 560 Geneva Road, Suite L2C
Carol Stream, IL 60188
630-221-1311
http://www.ispcan.org
Journal: *Child Abuse and Neglect: The International Journal*

National Association for Bilingual Education
Union Center Plaza
810 First Street, NE
Washington, DC 20002
http://www.nabe.org
Journal: *NABE Journal of Research and Practice*

National Association for Family Child Care
P.O. Box 10373
Des Moines, IA 50306
800-359-3817
http://www.nafcc.org
Journal: *The National Perspective*

National Black Child Development Institute
1023 15th Avenue, NW
Washington, DC 20002
202-833-2220
http://www.nbcdi.org

National Education Association (NEA)
1201 16th Street, NW
Washington, DC 20036
202-833-4000
http://www.nea.org
Journals: *Works4Me* and *NEA Focus,* by online subscription

National Head Start Association
1651 Prince Street
Alexandria, VA 22314
703-739-0875
http://www.nhsa.org
Journal: *Children and Families*

Zero to Three: National Center for Infants, Toddlers, and Families
2000 M. Street NW, Suite 200
Washington, DC 20036
202-638-1144
http://www.zerotothree.org
Journal: *Zero to Three*

# RESOURCES

## PLANNING ENVIRONMENTS FOR LITERACY

*Early Language and Literacy Classroom Observation* (ELLCO) *Toolkit,* Research Edition, by Miriam W. Smith, Ed.D., and David K. Dickinson, Ed.D., with Angela Sangeorge and Louisa Anastasopoulos, M.P.P.

ELLCO is a three-part classroom observation that helps teachers assess and strengthen literacy components and classroom quality.

*Literacy: The Creative Curriculum Approach,* by Cate Heroman and Candy Jones.

This book shows teachers how to create literacy learning opportunities within an integrated curriculum for children ages three to five. This book describes the seven components of literacy in detail: literacy as a source of enjoyment, vocabulary and language, phonological awareness, knowledge of print, letters and words, comprehension, and books and other texts. The book explains the basics of how to design a literacy program, how to plan activities and interactions, and how to use a continuum of literacy skills.

## LITERACY RESOURCE BOOKS FOR TEACHERS

*Early Childhood Experiences in Language Arts,* by Jeanne M. Machado.

This reference book can help teachers of young children understand the development of literacy and how teachers can plan for quality programs for young children.

*Growing Up with Literature,* by Walter E. Sawyer.

This book has good information on how to choose and share quality children's literature with young children. It is not an activity book, but it is a good reference book for use in the classroom.

*Peak with Books: An Early Childhood Resource for Balanced Literacy,* by Marjorie Nelsen and Jan Nelsen-Parish.

This book has numerous teaching ideas that center around some popular children's books, such as *Blueberries for Sal* and *Freight Train.*

*Seeing Young Children: A Guide to Observing and Recording Behavior,* by Warren Bentzen.

This detailed resource book describes the process of observation and how to use various observation techniques to assess children. This book also explains the differences in children from birth to school age and how to best observe children of various ages.

*Starting Out Right: A Guide to Promoting Children's Reading Success,* by the National Research Council.

Every teacher, parent, or child care provider should have a copy of this book because it is one of the few that gives an overview of activities, information, and resources for birth through second grade. Clearly written with a concise, easy-to-understand format, it is available from National Academy Press (800-624-6242).

## LITERACY WEB LINKS

### American Library Association
http://www.ala.org
For a listing of Caldecott award winners from 1938 to the present, select *Libraries and You,* then *Recommended Reading* and *Caldecott Medal.*

### Center for the Improvement of Early Reading Achievement
http://www.ciera.org
This Web site contains products, information, and research on successful strategies for improving early reading skills of young children.

### Children's Literacy Initiative
http://www.cliontheweb.org
Children's Literacy Initiative works to increase children's literacy skills and to foster a love of reading by providing professional development for teachers of prekindergarten through third grade.

## Children's Literature Web Guide

http://www.acs.ucalgary.ca

This Web site provides Internet resources related to books for young children. Highlights include discussion boards, quick reference, and additional links to other resources on literature. Search for "Doucette Library" and then choose *Children's Lit Web Guide* under *Web Links*.

## International Reading Association (IRA)

http://www.reading.org

This is the home page for the IRA. There are many resources for improving the quality of reading instruction.

## The Internet Public Library Youth Division

http://ipl.si.umich.edu

This Web site has a myriad of educational things for children to do. Choose *KidSpace*.

## New York Public Library.

http://kids.nypl.org

Choose the link to *100 Picture Books Everyone Should Know* for a listing.

## Partnerships for Inclusion

http://www.fpg.unc.edu

For a downloadable listing of selected books for preschoolers, select *Partnerships for Inclusion* under *More Requested Pages* and then choose *Products, Preschool Picks*.

## The Soho Center, National Children's Literacy Website

http://www.child2000.org

For 28 years, various children's literacy initiatives have been an important part of the Soho Center's activities. This site gives parents and providers some ideas to consider. Click the *Yes* button from the home page. Then select *National Children's Literacy Website* and click *Click Here to take a look*.

## Teaching Strategies

http://www.teachingstrategies.com

This Web site is the online home of the Creative Curriculum resources. It contains much information, including how to implement the curriculum, and has a wealth of products to order based on the Creative Curriculum.

## COMPUTER PROGRAMS

The following companies provide information on or the actual computer software and CD-ROMs to support literacy development.

**Disney Direct**
http://www.disneydirect.com
800-328-0368

- Disney Learning Kindergarten

- Disney Learning Preschool

- Mickey Mouse Toddler

- Winnie the Pooh Baby

- Winnie the Pooh Toddler

**Fog-ware**
606 North First Street
San Jose, CA 95112
http://home.fog-ware.com

- SmartStart—1st Grade

- SmartStart—Kindergarten

- SmartStart—Preschool

- SmartStart—Toddlers

**Software for Kids**
250 Baldwin Avenue, Suite 804
San Mateo, CA 94401

- Curious George Reads, Writes & Spells for Grades 1 & 2

- I Love Spelling

- Jumpstart Phonics

- Little Bear Toddler Discovery Adventure

- Sesame Street Elmo's Reading Basic

- Sesame Street Preschool

## Learning-Lighthouse
http://www.learninglighthouse.com

- Chicka Chicka Boom Boom

## Brighter Child Interactive
651 Lakeview Plaza Boulevard, Suite C
Worthington, OH 43085
http://www.brighterchild.com

- Caillou Alphabet Preschool

- Land Before Time: Preschool

- Land Before Time: Toddler

## Kids Click Software
888-219-9030
http://www.kidsclick.com

This Web site provides a variety of software options.

- Fisher Price

- Ready for School Toddler

## Ventura Educational Systems
P.O. Box 425
Grover Beach, CA 93483-0425
800-336-1022
http://www.venturaes.com

- Number and Letter Excelerator Preschool Vocabulary Activities

- Phonics & Reading Excelerator

- Preschool Excelerator Preschool Language Activities

## Riverdeep, Inc.
100 Pine Street, Suite 1900
San Francisco, CA 94111
http://www.riverdeep.net

- Carmen Sandiego Word Detective

- Destination Reading—Grade K-3

- Kid Pix Deluxe 4 for Schools

- Read, Write & Type

- Reader Rabbit Baby & Toddler

- Reader Rabbit Learn to Read with Phonics

- Reader Rabbit Phonics Books for the LeapPad Personal Learning Tool

- Reader Rabbit Phonics Reading Series Books

- Reader Rabbit Preschool

- Reader Rabbit Reading Builder for Schools

- Reader Rabbit Toddler

- Reading Milestones

- Stories & More Animal Friends

- Student Writing Center

**School Zone Publishing Company**
1819 Industrial Drive
Grand Haven, MI 49417
http:://www.schoolzone.com

- Alphabet Express Preschool

- Flash Action Software

**JumpStart Learning System**
Knowledge Adventure
800-871-2969
http://www.jumpstart.com

- JumpStart Advanced (programs sold individually for grades 1–6)

- JumpStart Advanced Kindergarten

- JumpStart Advanced Preschool

- JumpStart Advanced Toddler

- JumpStart Phonics

- JumpStart Reading with Karaoke

- JumpStart Spanish

- JumpStart Study Helpers Spelling Bee

**LeapFrog Programs**
866-334-LEAP (5327)
http://www.leapfrog.com

- LeapPad Plus Writing Learning System

- Preschool & Kindergarten Library

**Kutoka Interactive**
http://www.kutoka.com
Grades: 6–12

Provides interactive language learning.

- EazySpeak French (English to French)

- EazySpeak Spanish (English to Spanish)

- EazySpeak Espagnol (French to Spanish)

- EazySpeak Anglais (French to English)

**Smart Kids Software**
P.O. Box 590464
Houston, TX 77259-0464
http://www.smartkidssoftware.com

This Web site provides access to a variety of software for children ranging in age from 9 months to 13 years.

- Interactive storybooks

## REAL WORK

You are the teacher of a four-year-old preschool classroom. A parent comes to you one morning and says that he is concerned that his child is not doing "real work." He wants his daughter to bring home homework and worksheets so that he can work with her on her letters and numbers. He does not want to have his child playing around all day; he wants her to be ready for school.

### How will you respond to this parent?

Perhaps you could explain to this parent that children learn in many ways and that the best ways for them to learn is by doing. Help such parents to understand that children learn and retain more when they actually have meaningful interactive experiences with letters and numbers. Give examples of how you incorporate letters and numbers in the activities in learning centers. If you are using some type of continuum of skills report for each child, you can easily help the parent to understand where the child is in her understanding of literacy and mathematics. It is good to plan interactive and meaningful experiences for the parents to share at home with the children; these experiences should center on fun ways to review colors, numbers, and so forth. The use of environmental print, such as cereal labels, can provide good opportunities for learning.

### What could you do from the very beginning of the school year to help parents understand that children learn best through interaction with meaningful experiences?

Parents will better understand the interactive approach to learning if you plan a session at the beginning of the school year to have them experience learning in that way firsthand. For example, have several manipulative items and materials from several learning centers displayed. Explain to the parents what the children will be learning from each of these materials. If parents feel confident that you understand the developmental continuum of skills and if you show them how these skills can be learned in a hands-on and meaningful way, they will not insist on sit-down worksheets as the major mode of instruction.

### What resources or information will you share with the parent?

- Share the information from the course of study for the classroom or from the skill continuum that your state uses.

- Share the information from the joint position statement of NAEYC and the International Reading Association on the best practices to help children develop literacy skills.

- Make sure that you have a system for documenting progress for each child so that parents can visually see the progression of their child. Portfolios for each child can be an excellent tool.

## THE UNINVOLVED PARENT

You are the teacher in a classroom of young toddlers. You have studied and understand the importance of talking with young children and the value of what they learn from early experiences with books, language play, and scribbling. You have a parent who never acknowledges the child upon arriving or departing. There is no evidence of positive talk or interaction with the child. When you ask about the child's favorite story, the parent says that the child does not need to be around books or crayons because the child will only eat them.

### How will you explain the importance of early literacy experiences for young toddlers?

Explain to the parent that literacy skills begin very early for young children and that those early experiences with language, such as engaging in interactive language interchange, viewing books, scribbling/writing, and hearing the rhythm of language, are important for the literacy development of young children. Help them understand that the foundation for literacy, as well as other skills, is built when the child is young. If children love language and books at a young age, they will most likely develop better language skills as they grow up.

### What suggestions will you make to the parent to generate interest in doing some fun literacy activities with the child?

Use the listing of durable books from the Zero to Three organization to help parents select books that are easy to share with a toddler. If parents are uncomfortable giving the child writing tools, suggest that they use chubby crayons, which are nontoxic, with large pieces of paper taped to the table. Explain that young children write with large muscle actions in the early stages, so the paper will need to be large. Encourage parents to talk to the child during routine times, such as while driving or eating dinner. Explain that television viewing should not take the place of interactive conversations.

### What resources or information will you share?

- Share information from the Zero to Three organization about the early development of literacy.

- Show parents examples of literacy materials that they could safely and easily use with a young child.

- Consider making a take-home packet of activities that parents might use at home.

## BUT I CANNOT READ

You are a kindergarten teacher and often have send-home books for parents to share with their children. You have a child in your classroom whose grandparent has permanent custody of the child. The grandmother confides in you that she is not a good reader at all and feels uncomfortable reading the books to the child.

### What can you do to provide positive shared literacy experiences for this grandparent and child that will be enjoyable and comfortable for both of them?

If a parent or grandparent has limited literacy skills, he or she can still share simple picture books and wordless picture books with the child. The stories in these wordless picture books are carried through the pictures instead of the text. In this way the grandparent can discuss the pictures and the story can be made new and exciting every time.

### What resources or information will you share with the grandparent?

- Provide wordless picture books that can be sent home with the child.

- Provide books on tape for the child and the grandparent to enjoy together. (Make sure that the time to turn the page is signified by a sound of some type.)

- Send home materials that can be interactive, such as puzzles and matching games, which are built on the books used in class so that the child can get experiences with the books in ways beyond the readings done in class.

- Record books on tape yourself for the child and grandparent to share together.

- If the grandparent is interested, you can help him or her get in touch with a local community college that provides reading classes in the community.

## TO TEST OR NOT TO TEST

You are a kindergarten teacher who believes in the value of interactive learning and authentic assessment. You have portfolios for each of your children, and you regularly observed the children for their progress along the continuum of literacy development. The administrators are exerting a lot of pressure to use some type of standardized pencil-and-paper assessment so that there can be documented proof that the children are really learning what they are supposed to be learning.

### What are the important types of documentation that you should be gathering for each of your students?

It is important to begin with a good comprehensive curriculum that has a continuum of skills for young children. Many states have a course of study for kindergarten. There are also many commercial products that can assist you in understanding the sequence of skills and documenting development. The Creative Curriculum and The Work Sampling System are only a couple of the comprehensive systems available. It is important to collect work samples throughout the year to document learning in each of the developmental domains: cognitive, physical, social, emotional, and language. The work samples and observations that are collected for the portfolio should be related directly to the continuum that you are using. Work samples should be labeled and have comments attached so that the child's developmental progress according to the continuum can be easily understood.

### How will you organize this information so that it can be understood and so that it will show the child's best work?

Some type of system should be put into place that accomplishes two things:

1. There is an organized portfolio for each child.

2. There is a consistent method established for doing observations and for collecting work samples from each child on a regular basis so that no one is left out.

It works well if the major indicators from the continuum are posted so that they serve as a guide to the teachers and to the assistants during observation and planning. Using a plan such as taking the top four or five children from the roster and making sure that observation notes and documentation are done for those children that day can be helpful. During the next day, focus on the next four children as you continue through the roster.

A good system for gathering and transferring observation notes to the child's folder is to carry a small clipboard with sheets of adhesive mailing labels that are about 3 by 5 inches or smaller. The notes can be recorded on these labels and later affixed to the child's folder or work samples as appropriate. Remember to be sure that the notes actually reflect progress along the continuum and are not simply a collection of interesting things that happened that day. Good observation and assessment should drive the planning process for the children.

### What information will you share with the administrator?

The hope is that before you begin the year, there is already a discussion about the use of a curriculum that incorporates observation and assessment, organization of the environment, planning activities, and use of appropriate interactions with the children. If you keep accurate and detailed information on the children and you can show the obvious link between your planning and the children's needs, then most administrators will be pleased.

## BUT I DON'T WANT TO LOOK AT BOOKS

You are a preschool teacher of four-year-olds. The interest inventory that you had parents fill out at the start of the year suggested to you that a particular child has had little or no experience with books. The child watches high-action videos and plays video games for much of his time at home. While at school, the child moves quickly from one center to another. He does not seem to focus a lot on any one particular activity. The child avoids sitting down with a book, saying that it is boring.

### How will you motivate the child to be interested in literacy-type activities?

This child would most likely benefit from the use of short, interactive-type books that would involve some active participation. Books that have colorful pictures and rhythm would also spark interest. It would be good to use puppets and flannel board activities as well.

### How will you organize the book area to encourage all of the children to be interested in enjoying books together there?

Make sure that the books in the library area are rotated frequently and are attractively displayed in such a way that the covers can easily be seen. Place puppets and other props in the library area as well. The secret is to find what interests the children and to capitalize on that. Remember also to use books throughout all centers in the classroom.

### What information or resources would be helpful for this family?

The family should be helped to understand the importance of time spent together enjoying books. It would also be important to provide fun alternatives to video games. Book packs with games to be played at home can be an alternative. Plan a field trip to the library so that families can get library cards and find out more about the services the library offers.

## WATCHING FOR LITERACY?

Ms. Shipp uses the video camera to record her children's literacy behavior. The recordings can include the video taping of circle time, center time, group time, and/or independent student working sessions. During these interactions the students engage in events such as singing songs, reciting the alphabet, and reading and reciting stories and poems. Ms. Shipp also says that individual reading time, writing workshops, and sharing, as well as dramatic play events, have been recorded for assessment purposes on several occasions. Mr. Thomas, one of Ms. Shipp's students, disagrees with such a procedure, citing that he does not see the relevance and prefers that the practice ends.

- What would be your response?

- How would you justify such a practice?

- How could you help Mr. Thomas understand your choice to video tape the literacy behavior in your class?

Possible Solutions: It is not uncommon for teachers to capture many educational moments that occur throughout the day with children in a variety of ways. This practice is used for assessment purposes, which will be analyzed and used to direct needed changes. The teacher can use the valuable information gained by such taping to detect areas of needed focus as well as children's literacy development during times of interaction in the class. Conversation development and interaction among the children can be viewed from a different perspective. Share other ways you are using the data gathered to support learning for all children.

Acknowledge the parent's concerns. Try to determine what is at the heart of the parent's concern. If you are having trouble seeing it from the parent's perspective discuss this concern with your director or principal.

As a note of caution, be sure that all parents are well aware before any video taping is done. Parents of children being video taped should be notified in writing for permission to record their child during educational settings. Also, share this valuable information with parents at open house and conferences to ensure that all parties are aware and on the same page.

## IS JOURNAL WRITING REALLY NECESSARY IN KINDERGARTEN?

Sam complains openly each day when asked to write in his daily journal. His teacher received a letter from his mother requesting a conference to discuss the purpose behind requiring the children to write in a journal every day.

- How would you respond to this situation?

- What are your reasons for requiring daily journal entries?

Possible Solutions: Journal writing can be very fun for children of all ages, but it can also be a stressful encounter if too much emphasis is placed on this assignment. Review your expectations concerning this assignment to determine factors that may be contributing to Sam's stress. Make this a nonthreatening time of learning and reflection. Share relevant information with the parents, such as how important the use of journals is as part of the kindergarten curriculum. The use of journals supports a child's expression on given and self-sectioned topics. It also provides an opportunity for inventive spelling, which is a key step to writing as a child builds on letter sounds to spell words needed to express his or her thoughts.

## IT LOOKS LIKE PLAYING TO ME

Mrs. Jones has observed several times in her three-year-old's classroom. She often voices her concerns that it appears that no structured learning lessons occur during the time she observes and visits the classroom. Mrs. Jones states that when she visits her child's classroom, she only sees the children playing with puzzles, toys, blocks, sewing cards, and cutting and drawing materials. She voiced a desire to see real learning lessons in action. This is a particular concern because she wants her child to be ready for school and she especially desires that her child have correct and neat handwriting when the time comes for her to begin writing.

- How will you address this concern with Mrs. Jones?

- Do you think the events observed by Mrs. Jones are age appropriate and provide learning opportunities for her students? Why or why not?

- Does Mrs. Jones have cause for concern?

Possible Solutions: It is assumed that all parents desire the best for their child. Mrs. Jones does not seem to understand why the children are taking part in the activities she observes upon visiting the classroom. Her main concern seems to be that her child will be ready for school in the coming years. She also expressed a concern with her daughter's developing handwriting. To put things in perspective, share relevant information with Mrs. Jones by discussing the importance of centers and learning opportunities to build not only prewriting skills but other developmental skills for this age group. Specifically, prewriting skills are acquired through the building of a children's fine and gross motor skill. Planning and scheduling activities that allow children to sew, cut, tear, draw, and manipulate puzzles and blocks will strengthen a child's fine and gross motor skills, thus building prewriting skills. When the time for handwriting development occurs, the previous learning opportunities will build a child's handwriting skills. Share other ways you can support handwriting and other skills in your class on a daily basis. Finally, remind Mrs. Jones that acquiring education is a journey and not a race. Thus, encourage her to join you in celebrating this season of learning in her child's life.

## HOW IMPORTANT ARE THE LETTERS?

Ms. Martin, a preschool teacher, is a new teacher at the school. She has voiced her concern that her current students are not readily grasping new information, mainly the recognition of the alphabet, as the students in all of her previous teaching encounters. Ms. Martin now overemphasizes the recognition of the alphabet in her classroom. She often becomes very upset when encouraged by other teachers to relax her emphasis on insisting that the children memorize too many letters in a week. It is obvious that this practice is now causing stress among the children; the children are no longer eager to work with Ms. Martin but prefer to interact with the other teacher in the class.

- Do you agree that Ms. Martin is placing too much emphasis on the recognition of the alphabet?

- What, if anything, could be the underlying reason for Ms. Martin's concern?

- How would you handle this situation?

Possible Solutions: To put emphasis on the recognition of the alphabet is a necessary step in building literary skills. Teachers are key facilitators in building and/or supplementing this necessary skill for children at an early age. However, overemphasizing must not be a part of this learning opportunity.

Ms. Martin is clearly overfocusing on necessary skills that will benefit her students if they are introduced and taught correctly. Possibly the underlying reasons for Ms. Martin's overemphasizing the alphabet could be her need to ensure that all of her students know such valuable information needed to support their future learning. Another perspective could be that Ms. Martin sees the students' failure to comprehend as a personal reflection on her teaching abilities. Many factors can play into her decision to over-force this skill. However, the concern must be addressed to prevent further diminishing her relationship with her students. Ms. Martin should be encouraged to avoid making verbal comparisons of her current students with those of her past teaching experiences. The other teacher in the class has a legitimate right to address this concern with the teacher in a respectful manner. The center director or school administrator should supply necessary additional support if problems persist.

# ISSUES AND TRENDS

## CURRENT REALITIES OF TWENTY-FIRST CENTURY*

- Elementary schools are becoming overcrowded by the children of the baby boom generation. The U.S. Department of Education has predicted that elementary school enrollment will be at 54.6 million by the end of the current year (2006).

- The number of children from poverty and whose first language is not English will continue to rise. According to the National Center for Educational Statistics, the number of Hispanic children ages 5 to 13 will rise by 47 percent between 2000 and 2020.

- The teacher shortage is becoming critical; 30 percent of teachers leave the profession after 3 years. The large number of teachers retiring is also a major factor in the shortage. The U.S. Department of Education predicts that the educational system will need 190,000 additional teachers to meet the current demand.

- Most teachers entering the field of education are still mostly middle-class white females. The increasing diversity of children in today's classrooms gives rise to an even greater need to recruit greater diversity in those who teach.

- The literacy demands of the future will go far beyond what is required in today's society. This is a great challenge, especially in light of the concerns regarding literacy rates today.

---

*Adapted from Robinson, R., McKenna, M. C., & Wedman, J. W. (2004). *Issues and trends in literacy education*. Boston: Pearson Allyn and Bacon.

## NO CHILD LEFT BEHIND

The federal legislation referred to as the No Child Left Behind Act has had many implications for teacher education and accountability. As a result of this legislation, all teachers and paraprofessionals must be considered highly qualified in order to teach children. Therefore, professional development opportunities that focus on college credit in the areas of certification have increased. This legislation is one factor that points to the truth that teaching is a growing and changing field and that, as teachers, we must always continue to learn how to do our jobs even better.

## INCREASED EMPHASIS ON UNDERGRADUATE EDUCATION WITH A FOCUS ON THE EARLY YEARS

With the improved findings from brain research, which highlight the importance of learning in the early years, there has been a greater emphasis on increasing the educational level of child care providers who have a direct impact on the child and his or her family during the early years. Many states are implementing higher educational requirements for those who teach and care for our youngest citizens. Because of these initiatives, there is more scholarship money for child care providers to return to school. Because research shows that a major indicator of quality in early childhood programs is related to the level of education of the teacher, many states have licensing ratings, which take teacher education as a part of the formula.

Another outgrowth of the push for quality programs for young children and for quality teacher educational preparation programs for those who teach young children, the NAEYC is beginning a program of national accreditation for 2-year teacher education programs. This will be important as 4-year institutions consider articulating credit from these 2-year programs for teachers who wish to continue working toward a 4-year degree.

## EMPHASIS ON LITERACY EDUCATION WITH A FOCUS ON THE EARLY YEARS

Most experts in the area of reading and literacy are suggesting that reading failure can be prevented in most cases if successful programs for early screening and remediation are in place. Remediation after the second grade is usually not as effective as the programs that begin earlier. Failure in learning to read is devastating for a young child. Therefore, literacy has been brought to the forefront as a primary focus for education. Terms such as *print-rich environments, positive talk environments,* and *early intervention* are beginning to become common in the early childhood realm. It is important that teachers of young children and child care providers have a good understanding of how literacy understanding and competence develop. As a result of this, many states are requiring both teachers and paraprofessionals to complete one or more courses in literacy education as a part of their educational requirements.

Because all children are different and they learn differently, there is no one-size-fits-all answer. Understanding how to observe and assess children's understandings has become a crucial part of the planning process. As teachers of young children, we must understand the continuum of literacy skills and we must carefully plan environments and activities that support and enhance literacy skills for all children.

## MEETING THE NEEDS OF AT-RISK LEARNERS

Because the early years of a child's life are crucial to educational potential during later years, more emphasis has been placed on meeting the needs of at-risk learners. There have even been lawsuits leveraged against states because of the belief that at-risk children did not receive adequate early educational opportunities in order to begin school ready to succeed. Many states have put programs into place to enhance educational opportunities for children who are identified as being at risk. The earlier children are exposed to books and language, the better. The idea is not to push babies to create "superbabies" but rather to provide quality environments that support the development of language and literacy.

## FOCUS ON FAMILY LITERACY

The family is the first and most important teacher of young children. Young children cannot reach their potential unless there is a close partnership between the schools and the families. Several programs have been created with the goal of developing early partnerships with families. A few of these are listed here:

Even Start: This is a federally funded family literacy program. The goal is that children participate in quality education opportunities while parents are increasing their own educational level through the acquisition of their high school equivalency or General Educational Diploma.

Parents as Teachers: This organization trains professionals to work with families of young children in an effort to help them improve their parenting skills and to help them understand how to enhance educational opportunities for their children.

Mother Read: This program trains professionals to help parents use good children's literature as a way to improve the literacy skills of young children. The hope is that the literacy skills of parents will be increased through the use of good literature and that the parents will understand how to share good books with their children.

The International Reading Association has made the following suggestions for successful partnerships between schools and children:

- Be aware of the importance of quality family-school connections.

- Think systematically about attitudes toward family involvement.

- Understand that different types of family involvement can be effective. Carefully consider the goals, benefits, and barriers of each type.

- Be aware of the role that culture and life experiences play in the way in which a family operates.

- Be able to build on family diversity.

- Be able to include and work with other professionals in an effort to help families.

- Be willing to assume responsibility for establishing and maintaining the partnership with families.

## LET'S LIFT LITERARY

To strengthen and develop our children in the area of literacy continues to be a very important priority of parents and educators today. As this emphasis remains a center focus, support literacy in the following ways.

The benefits of books at an early age must be supported and promoted by teachers and parents. Therefore, provide books for all ages. It is never too early to start reading and exposing children as young as infants to book. Even reading to the fetus has scientific benefits. Even before a child can read, exposure to books still provides many beneficial factors. For instance, exposure to books for babies provides an interesting opportunity for them to explore sensory awareness through touch and focusing on the color and printed materials on the book itself. Regardless of a child's age, the use of and exposure to books will expand his or her creativity, imagination, and overall literary development.

## DEVELOPMENTALLY APPROPRIATE PRACTICE FOR LITERACY EDUCATION

Overemphasizing literacy development before a child is ready can affect the child's future learning desires and goals. The learning environment and motivations to read, write, speak, and listen in depth must be emphasized with purpose and meaning, without pressure.

Safeguarding child self-esteem is necessary for the development of the whole child. Children develop at their own rates in areas of development. The interaction a child has with his or her parent and teachers will influence language development in that child. Build on opportunities for the children to communicate openly.

## COMPUTER AND LITERARY

The use of computers will supplement the learning outcomes of children in many ways. Computer options provide students of all ages with individualized learning encounters and opportunities to gain valuable knowledge. Programs that reinforce concepts by providing immediate feedback strengthen a child's desire to learn. In addition, interactive computer programs reinforce teacher-taught objectives and concepts.

The use of computers has many benefits to the learner. Supporting and supplementing literary development is one such benefit. Many computer programs, as well as the use of the computer itself, will influence a child's literary development. Children enjoy writing, editing, and publishing their written works using the computer.

# NOTES

# NOTES

# NOTES

# NOTES

# NOTES

# NOTES

# NOTES

# NOTES